A BRIEFER HISTORY OF TIME

A BRIEFER HISTORY OF TIME

FROM THE BIG BANG TO THE BIG MAC®

Eric Schulman

W. H. Freeman and Company
New York

Illustration of Cambrian Earth, p. © C. Scotese. Used by permission.
Hubble Space Telescope photos pp. 17-23 are reproduced with permission from AURA/STScI
Illustration of dinosaur, p 62 © *Annals of Improbable Research*. Grateful permission for use is acknowledged.
Illustration of weather map, p. 71 © me.

ISBN 0-7167-3389-7

Library of Congress Cataloging-in-Publication Data available upon request

Printed in the United States of America

First printing 1999

This book is dedicated to Emily

I don't pretend to understand the Universe—it's a great deal bigger than I am.

—Thomas Carlyle, December 28, 1868

A BRIEFER HISTORY OF TIME
The History of the Universe in 100 Words or Less

Quantum fluctuation. Inflation. Expansion. Particle-antiparticle annihilation. Deuterium and helium production. Recombination. Galaxy formation. Turbulent fragmentation. Massive star formation. Stellar evolution. Iron production. Supernova explosion. Star formation. Planetary differentiation. Volatile gas expulsion. Molecular reproduction. Protein construction. Fermentation. Cell differentiation. Respiration. Multicellular organisms. Sexual reproduction. Evolutionary diversification. Trilobite domination. Land exploration. Comet collision. Dinosaur extinction. Mammal expansion. Homo sapiens manifestation. Language acquisition. Glaciation. Innovation. Religion. Animal domestication. Food surplus production. Inscription. Warring nations. Empire creation and destruction. Civilization. Constitution. Industrialization. World conflagrations. Fission explosions. Computerization. Population Explosion. Space exploration. Superpower confrontation. Internet expansion. Resignation. Reunification. World Wide Web creation. Composition. Extrapolation.

A NOT-QUITE-SO BRIEF HISTORY OF TIME

PREFACE

I decided to try to write a popular book about the history of the universe after I participated in the Seventh First Annual Ig Nobel Prize Ceremony at Harvard University in 1997. A considerable number of such books had already been written, of course, ranging from the very informative and humorous, such as Larry Gonick's *The Cartoon History of the Universe*, to the not-so-informative or -humorous, which I will not identify. However, I felt that none of them really addressed the questions that had led me to study science in the first place: Where are we now? Where have we been? Is there an amusing and informative way of describing the journey? These questions are of interest to us all,
or at least to all of us reading this particular book.

This century has seen scientific fields becoming so complex that only a small number of specialists are able to master their techniques and the mathematics used to describe them. And very few of these people have the time and inclination to write amusing books describing the highlights, not only of their own field, but also of other relevant fields. That is what I have attempted to do in this book. It is up to the reader to judge whether I have succeeded.

I read somewhere that each equation included in a popular science book will halve the sales, but that this effect does not occur with Einstein's famous equation $E=mc^2$. Can you guess which equation I included in this book?

In reading this book you will probably encounter some terms with which you are unfamiliar. You will not be tested on these terms, but if you wish to review them, then feel free to use the extensive glossary at the end of the book.

Each of the fifty-three chapters in this book represents a significant event in the history of the universe. The first page of each chapter lets you know where and when the event occurred. Time points early in the history of the universe give the time elapsed since the Big Bang—these are usually written in scientific notation. You can look at the glossary entry on "scientific notation" for more information on how to interpret these numbers.

Thank you for buying this book. (If you are just browsing, please reread this sentence after you purchase it; if you have checked it out of the library, please thank the librarian and suggest that extra copies be ordered.) I hope that you enjoy it, that you learn from it, and that you recommend it to friends, relatives, coworkers, acquaintances, bartenders, bus drivers, flight attendants, random passers-by, and pretty much anyone else you happen to meet.

Eric Schulman
Alexandria, Virginia
16th December 1998

QUANTUM FLUCTUATION

In Which

the Universe Begins

---

nce upon a time, long ago and far away, there was a universe very much like our own. It had dogs, and cats, and people (some of whom preferred the dogs and some of whom preferred the cats), and Trigoence-phalopodic Gnoccis, and other things that you've never heard of because we haven't encountered them yet.

Like our own universe, this one was infinite in size. And one interesting thing about infinite universes, is that anything that has even a slight chance of happening will be happening somewhere, even if the probability is very small.

Now it just so happened that one of the effects of quantum mechanics is that large amounts of matter and energy could spontaneously appear, even though this rarely happened in a given volume of space.* Well, on this particular once-upon-a-time, an entire universe appeared. Its density was more than 1,000 billion billion billion billion billion billion billion billion billion billion times that of water, and its temperature was more than 100,000 billion billion billion degrees Fahrenheit. Immediately, it began to expand, become

*While it is a fundamental assumption of physics that the laws governing the universe remain unchanged, it is also a fundamental tenet of fairy tales that they be told in the past tense.

less dense, and cool off. Luckily for the inhabitants of the first universe, the new universe quickly became detached from the old universe and started expanding into a completely different four-dimensional volume of space.

This is the story of that universe, and of some of the things that have happened in it during the last 15 billion years.

INFLATION

In Which
the Grand Unified Force Separates into the Four Forces of Nature as We Now Know Them, and the Universe Expands to Many Times Its Original Size in a Very Short Period of Time

---

"Welcome ladies and gentlemen to another beautiful diurnal period here at Universal Downs. We're ready for the start of what should be a most exciting Cosmological Derby. There are just four forces competing today, but each and every one of them is champion in its own right.

"In the starting position it's Gravity, next is Strong Nuclear, then Weak Nuclear, and finally a young filly named Electromagnetism. All four forces are lined up and unified at the starting gate, waiting for the bell to announce the moment of the Big Bang, which will start this exciting race to determine which is the strongest force in the universe.

"There's the starting bell, and they're off!

"At 10^{-43} seconds it's Weak Nuclear neck and neck with Electromagnetism and Strong Nuclear force, with Gravity bringing upthe rear.

"It's still a little early in the race folks, just 10^{-38} seconds, but it looks like Strong Nuclear might be making its move. Yes, at 10^{-37} seconds Strong Nuclear has broken away from Electromagnetism and Weak Nuclear!

"The energy density is astounding, ladies and gentlemen, the universe is expanding exponentially! This is turning out to be a real donnybrook!!

"We're at 10^{-36} seconds and it's still going. 10^{-35} seconds. 10^{-34} seconds . . . .

"Oh wait, wait . . . what's this? It's 10^{-33} seconds and I think . . . I think . . . yes indeed, ladies and gentlemen! The transition to broken symmetry is complete at 10^{-32} seconds.

"Strong Nuclear is now about fourteen times stronger than Electromagnetism, and the universe is more than a billion billion billion billion billion billion times larger than it was at 10^{-37} seconds.

"The crowd is going wild—they're throwing their sombreros into the air and shouting, "Higgs! Higgs! Higgs!"* Such a magnificent showing by Strong Nuclear! What a force!

*The four forces separated due to a process called "spontaneous symmetry-breaking," caused by a "Higgs field" whose "potential" is sort of "sombrero-shaped." While the fundamental particle physicists frown at the lack of precision in this explanation, the rest of us may continue on to the next chapter, which discusses parking places.

EXPANSION

In Which
the Universe Continues to Expand,
Though not Quite as Quickly

The universe is expanding. And yet for some reason it never gets any easier to find a parking place. There are a couple of reasons for this. First, the universe is expanding very slowly: You would have to wait 65 million years for a one-mile block in the middle of space to expand enough to produce another parking space.* The other reason is that the gravitational attraction between all of the particles in the Earth completely overcomes the expansion of the universe, so even if you circled a block on Earth for 65 million years it wouldn't get any bigger. Taking public transportation would be a much more efficient use of your time.

But if the universe is expanding, what is it expanding into? In order to answer that question, let us imagine ourselves to be two-dimensional creatures living on the surface of a balloon. The only directions we know are backwards/forwards and right/left. Only the mathematicians among us have any concept of up/down, and everyone suspects that they are just making it up. Eventually however, some two-dimensional astronomers discover that the balloon is expanding, but how could that be? To an outside—

---

* There are some who say that it would take only 50 million years and others who claim that it would take 80 million years, but take my word for it, you'd be waiting 65 million years.

that is to say, three-dimensional—observer it would be obvious: the balloon is increasing in volume and the surface of the balloon—the two-dimensional "universe"—is increasing in area. However, these concepts are quite difficult for the two-dimensional inhabitants of balloonland.

So am I saying that our universe is like a three-dimensional balloon expanding into a four-dimensional space? Well . . . maybe. But that would imply that the universe has a finite volume—astronomers call this type of universe "closed"—and that it will eventually stop expanding and begin to recollapse. While this is possible, many astronomers now consider it to be unlikely.

So what is the universe really like? It appears most likely that the universe is infinite in extent—"open"—and will continue to expand forever, which implies that it is a three-dimensional hyperbolic paraboloid in four-dimensional space. Think of it as the four-dimensional representation of a three-dimensional saddle. Or, better yet, try not to worry about it at all. It won't make it any easier to find a parking place.

PARTICLE-ANTIPARTICLE ANNIHILATION

In Which
**All the Antiparticles in the Universe Annihilate Almost
All the Particles, Creating a Universe Made Up of Matter
and Photons**

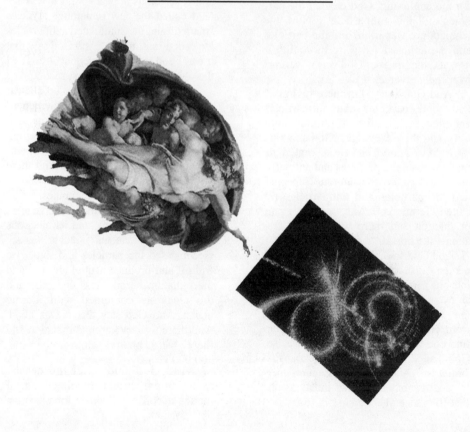

THE FIRST BOOK OF GAMOV, CALLED

ORIGINS

CHAPTER 1
In which the universe is created.

In the beginning, God created the particles and the antiparticles[a]. Now the temperature was high, and the particles and the antiparticles were in equilibrium, and the Spirit of God was hovering[b] over the Universe.

2 And God said, "Let there be light," and some particles and antiparticles annihilated each other to produce photons, and there was light. God saw that the light was good, and He separated the photons from the particles and antiparticles. God called the photons "bosons" and the particles and antiparticles He called "fermions."[c] And there was pair production and there was photon creation—the first 10^{-43} seconds

3 And God said, "Let there be an exponential expansion of the universe to separate one part from another." So God made an exponential expansion of the universe that separated the magnetic monopoles from each other so that all attempts to find one would be futile. And it was so. God called the exponential expansion "inflation." And there was vacuum energy density and there was inflation—the first 10^{-32} seconds.

4 And God said, "Let the antiparticles and the particles be gathered together, and let photons appear." And it was so. God called the few remaining particles "matter," and the annihilated antiparticles He called "antimatter." And God saw that it was good. And there were neutrons and there were protons—the first second.

5 And God said, "Let there be nuclear reactions to produce heavier elements." And it was so. God made protons and neutrons combine to produce deuterium nuclei, and the deuterium nuclei He combined to make helium nuclei. And there was some lithium and there was some beryllium—the first three minutes.

6 And God said, "Let the Universe teem with energetic photons, and let electrons fly past atomic nuclei." And it was so. God blessed the particles and said, "Be fruitful and produce neutral atoms," and the radiation became less energetic and the electrons combined with atomic nuclei. And God saw that it was good. And there was background radiation and there were neutral atoms—the first 300,000 years.

7 And God said, "Let the density perturbations produce collections of matter according to their kinds: stars,

a Antiparticles are very much like particles, except that when particles and antiparticles meet they completely destroy each other and emit a burst of energetic radiation.

b In a four dimensional sense; God does move in mysterious ways sometimes.

c He called some of the particles and antiparticles bosons as well, but that's another story.

galaxies, and clusters of galaxies, each according to its kind." And it was so. God made the clusters of galaxies according to their kinds, and the galaxies according to their kinds, and the stars according to their kinds. And God saw that it was good.

8 Then God said, "Let us make gravity in our image, in our likeness, and let it rule over the superclusters of galaxies, over the clusters of galaxies, over the groups of galaxies, over the galaxies, over the clusters of stars, and over the solar systems."

9 God saw all that He had made and it was very good. And there was violent relaxation and virialization—the first billion years

10 By the first billion years God had finished the work He had been doing; so after the first billion years He rested from all His work. And God blessed the remaining time in the universe, and made it holy, because during it He rested from all the work of creating that He had done.

DEUTERIUM AND HELIUM PRODUCTION

In Which
Many of the Protons and Neutrons in the Early Universe
Combine to Form Heavy Hydrogen and Helium

———————————

The Taming of the Neutrino

THE PERSONS OF THE PLAY

PETRUCHIO, a proton
GRUMIO, a neutron
PETRUMIO, a deuteron
HORTENSIO, a deuteron
PETRUMSIO, a helium nucleus

ACT I

Scene 1: *Padua. A public place. Before the spatial domain of* HORTENSIO.

    Enter PETRUCHIO *and* GRUMIO

PETRUCHIO   Verona, for a while I take my leave,
To see my friends in Padua; but, of all,
My best belovéd and approvéd friend,
Hortensio; and I trow this is his spatial domain---
    Here, sirrah Grumio; knock, I say.

GRUMIO   Knock, sir! Whom should I knock? Is there any
    particle has rebused your worship?

PETRUCHIO   Villain, I say, knock me here soundly.

GRUMIO   Knock you here, sir? Why, sir, what am I, sir, that
I should knock you here, sir?

PETRUCHIO   Villain, I say, knock me at this energy barrier,   10
And rap me well, or I'll knock your knave's hair.

[GRUMIO *tunnels through* PETRUCHIO'S *energy barrier, producing*
PETRUMIO, *a deuteron.*]

Enter HORTENSIO.

HORTENSIO: How now! What's the matter? My old friend Grumio
and my good friend Petruchio! How came you from Verona
and into Petrumio!

[PETRUMIO tunnels through HORTENSIO'S energy barrier,
producing PETRUMSIO, a helium nucleus.
[Exit PETRUMSIO]

RECOMBINATION

In Which
Electrons Combine with Hydrogen
and Helium Nuclei, Producing Neutral Atoms

---

*"Okay atoms,
let's get ready
to do the
Recombination
Dance!"*

Allemande left, photon hits on you,
Electron escapes; now you're through.
One on the right comes to your aid,
Meet new electron: promenade!

While photons hot, electrons gone,
If photons cold, electrons come,
The Universe expands and cools,
Join your partner: obey the rules!

With photons flying far and wide,
Keep your electrons by your side.
While you may think this dance is square,
Fusion is coming, so take care.

You'll have a billion years of calm,
Before galaxies start to form.
But once the stars begin to shine,
You'll be missin' this peaceful time.

GALAXY FORMATION

In Which
the Milky Way Galaxy Forms

THE DAILY UNIVERSE

MONDAY, JUNE 21, 10,000,000 B.C.

MAJOR GALAXY FORMS IN THE UNFASHIONABLE LOCAL GROUP

Could life develop there?

LOCAL GROUP, 10 billion years B.C.—Another major galaxy formed today in the Local Group, a collection of about two dozen galaxies located on the outskirts of the large Virgo Cluster of Galaxies. The new spiral galaxy has a mass of 500 billion

Continued on Page A2

solar masses (a solar mass is equivalent to 4000 billion billion billion pounds) and a diameter of 100,000 light years (a light year is the distance that light travels in a year, about 6 trillion miles); it is the second large galaxy to form in the Local Group in the past 100 million years. Whether life will develop within either of these galaxies is currently an open question.

"The first stars formed just after the pre-galactic cloud began to collapse, and many of them reside in one of the hundreds of globular clusters in the new galaxy," one observer reported. Globular clusters contain hundreds of thousands of stars and orbit the new galaxy along elliptical paths. The stars here are mostly hydrogen and helium, so it is not expected that many planets will form, making it unlikely for life to arise around these stars.

As the pre-galactic cloud began to collapse in earnest, the cloud's slight rotation became faster and faster and the stars and gas formed a disk. "This thin layer of stars and gas looks like a phonograph record and is rotating around the center of the galaxy at a speed of about half a million miles per hour," says another expert. It is expected that the intense star formation in this region of the new galaxy will result in large amounts of the elements needed to form planets and life.

The chances for life may be highest near the center of the galaxy, where the star formation is most intense. However, it is possible that supernova explosions will sterilize planets that orbit stars close to the center of the galaxy. When asked to rate the chances of the first life in this galaxy arising as far away as 30,000 light-years from the center of the galaxy, most experts estimated the probability to be "absurdly small."

TURBULENT FRAGMENTATION

In Which
a Giant Cloud of Gas Fragments into
Smaller Clouds, Which Become Protostars

a stellar nursery

TEXT BY ERIC R. SCHULMAN   PHOTOGRAPHS BY HUBBLE S. TELESCOPE

IF YOU'RE LIKE ME, YOU'VE PROBABLY LOOKED UP AT THE SKY COUNTLESS TIMES TO ADMIRE THE BEAUTIFUL starry night and wished you could have the same effect on the ceiling in your kitchen. You can! Because this month's issue of *Martha Stellar Living* is devoted to learning how to make a star. I love stars because they provide an opportunity to be so wonderfully creative with such simple ingredients. The variations are endless! That cloud of gas you probably

Stars!
(part 1)

have in your garden could be turned into an old standby such as a Sun-like yellow star. And by simply adding a bit of mass you can easily produce a brilliant blue supergiant. It's just the nature of stars, and it's one of the many reasons I never tire of making them!

Of course, a well-stocked pantry makes the preparation of stars much, much simpler. The ingredients, for the most part, are not expensive. Magnetic fields are most important and a good garden is an absolute must for providing the necessary elements. My garden is modest,

FACING PAGE: Stars as far as the eye can see—and you can make them at home using simple materials.

only a few cubic parsecs in size—about 100,000 billion billion billion billion billion cubic yards or so—but it provides me with all the hydrogen, helium, and trace elements necessary to make perfect stars every time.

To start, take a cloud with about ten thousand solar masses of material. The cloud will be rotating, from the entire cloud to the surrounding medium. Don't rush this step—you need to wait a full million or even ten million years before proceeding if you want a perfect star. You can put this time to good use though: there's always plenty to do around the house and lots of suggestions can be found in my new book, *Martha Stellar's Helpful*

ABOVE: **The classic steps in star formation—from left to to right, a cloud of gas condenses to form a protostar. Don't rush here: time makes the perfect star!**

which is a problem because of course angular momentum is conserved. This is often very troubling to novices since the traditional methods won't help here, but remember that flexibility is an important part of being a good and creative cook. So instead of dealing with each part of the cloud individually, add a magnetic field to transfer some of the angular momentum

Hints for Heavenly Households.

Your cloud should be relatively smooth now, with just a few lumps here and there. We're almost finished: At this point, just add some random motion to the mixture, and watch as the turbulence fragments it into smaller and smaller pieces. Each one of these pieces can be turned into a perfect star—I'll show you how to do that in part 2. ■

MASSIVE STAR FORMATION

In Which
a Massive Star Is Formed

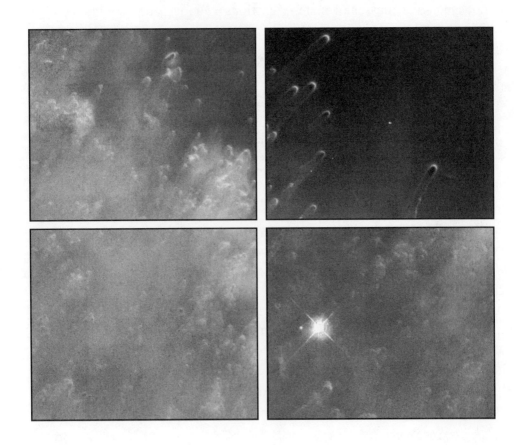

stars in the making

TEXT BY ERIC R. SCHULMAN   PHOTOGRAPHS BY HUBBLE S. TELESCOPE

IN PART 1, I SHOWED YOU HOW TO TURN A GIANT MOLECULAR CLOUD INTO SOME LOVELY PROTOSTARS, AND now we're going to learn how to turn one of these into a perfect star.

It is imperative that your protostar be cool, between -440 and -445 degrees Fahrenheit (that's between 8 and 11 Kelvin for you absolute temperature scale fans). As long as you keep it transparent, the radiation will escape from the center and the temperature will be stable. Remember that you can't get a perfect star if it is heated unevenly during formation, so never skimp on these details.

Stars!
(part 2)

FACING PAGE: **Clouds of gas can become beautiful stellar bouquets in a few million years—it's easier than you think!**

After a few thousand years, the central regions should become dense and begin to collapse faster than the rest. The density and pressure should increase until the central regions reach a temperature of about 3,140 degrees Fahrenheit, at which point the hydrogen molecules (H_2) begin to break into hydrogen atoms, spurring further collapse until a temperature of about 53,540 degrees Fahrenheit is reached in the core. This increase in core temperature should occur over a period of a few hundred thousand years —remember not to rush things— and the surface temperature will increase from -270 degrees Fahrenheit to a most satisfactory 4,940 degrees Fahrenheit.

April 8,990,000,000 B.C.

21

At this point, the time needed for the next step depends greatly on the final mass you want the star to have. Because I insist on offering only the very best to my guests, I usually make a massive star of about 15 solar masses. And since such stars don't take as long to make, I can create more of them. While a star the mass of the sun would take 40 million years to complete the protostar phase, a 15 solar mass star needs only 60,000 years. Of course, the more massive star will live for only 10 million years rather than 10 billion, but that can be an advantage since I like to redecorate fairly frequently. Also, the more massive star is more luminous (by a factor of 21,000), hotter (60,000 degrees Fahrenheit rather than 10,000), and has a larger diameter (by a factor of 10). Still, since less massive stars are cool, they are also red, and I sometimes make a number of low mass stars just for a little variety in color. Remember, the star clusters you create can be elaborate, elegant, and quite substantial at the same time.

Don't forget that the final mass of each star will depend somewhat on the environment of the protostar. Therefore, you'll want to prepare the region ahead of time so there will be no errors.

We're about ready to finish up now. There are just a few more details. In the final stages, the core temperature increases to a few hundred thousand degrees Fahrenheit, the hydrogen is ionized, and then the star contracts to its final radius. Once the core temperature is high enough (millions of degrees Fahrenheit), nuclear fusion commences, and a new star is born. Remember that throughout this process, organization is of utmost importance. Make sure that your ingredients are ready when they are needed. Knowing when and where to add more material is absolutely essential for making a perfect star. If the star rotates too quickly, it could end up with an active surface, and it will not make for a lovely presentation. And with stars, as with so many other things in life, presentation makes perfect! ■

STELLAR EVOLUTION

In Which
Stars Evolve and Eventually Die

OK STELLAR RECRUITS, IT'S TIME TO LEARN WHAT'S REALLY IN STORE FOR YOU! I KNOW THAT BEFORE YOU SIGNED UP TO BE A MASSIVE STAR YOU READ THE *FANCY* BROCHURES THAT TALKED ABOUT HOW *BRIGHTLY* YOU'D BE SHINING AND HOW YOU'D BE VISIBLE FROM HALFWAY ACROSS THE GALAXY. BUT YOU MO-RONS MUST NOT HAVE BOTHERED TO READ THE FINE PRINT THAT SAID THAT YOU'D EXPLODE IN SEVEN MILLION YEARS! AND IF YOU DID READ IT THEN YOU'RE EVEN STUPIDER THAN YOU LOOK. SEVEN MILLION YEARS IS NOT A LONG TIME!

NOW YOU'RE BURNING HYDROGEN TO HELIUM DEEP INSIDE YOU AND YOUR CORE IS GETTING DENSER AND DENSER. AFTER THAT LITTLE SEVEN MILLION YEAR VACATION IS OVER, YOU POOR SLOBS WILL HAVE USED UP ALL THE HYDROGEN CLOSE TO YOUR CENTER. YOUR CORE WILL COLLAPSE UNDER ITS OWN SICKENING WEIGHT UNTIL IT BECOMES HOT ENOUGH TO START FUS-ING HELIUM. MEANWHILE, OUTSIDE THE CORE YOU

SHRINKING VIOLETS WILL CONTRACT UNTIL THE HYDRO-
GEN THERE IS HOT ENOUGH TO FUSE. YOU KNOW WHAT
WILL HAPPEN TO THE ENERGY FROM ALL THIS FUSION?
IT'LL GET TRANSMITTED TO YOUR OUTER LAYERS AND
YOU'LL SWELL UP TO 100 TIMES YOUR ORIGINAL SIZE.

AFTER THAT YOU HAVE LESS THAN A MILLION
YEARS BEFORE YOU GO OUT WITH A BANG AS A SUPER-
NOVA. IF YOU'RE LUCKY YOU'LL WIND UP BEING A NEU-
TRON STAR, BUT KNOWING YOUR TYPE YOU'LL PROBABLY
END UP AS A BLACK HOLE AND TURN INTO A SINGUL-
ARITY OF INFINITE DENSITY AND ZERO VOLUME. YOU
RECRUITS ACT LIKE YOU'RE ALMOST DENSE ENOUGH
ALREADY.

YOU COULD HAVE CHOSEN TO BE A LOWER-MASS
STAR, YOU KNOW. THEN YOUR HYDROGEN WOULD HAVE
LASTED BILLIONS OR TRILLIONS OF YEARS. YOU'D STILL
GO THROUGH A GIANT PHASE, BUT AFTER FUSING HEL-
IUM TO CARBON YOU'D SETTLE DOWN AND SLOWLY COOL
OFF AS A WHITE DWARF. NOW THAT'S A PLEASANT
RETIREMENT.

OF COURSE, KNOWING YOU, YOU'D PROBABLY
HAVE HUNG OUT WITH SOME LOOSE STAR, GOTTEN TOO
MUCH MASS FROM THEM AND BEEN COMPLETELY DIS-
RUPTED IN A SUPERNOVA EXPLOSION. YOUR TYPE
MAKES ME SICK! OK, ENOUGH CHATTER, TIME FOR YOU
TO USE THOSE ULTRAVIOLET PHOTONS OF YOURS TO
CLEAN UP THIS MOLECULAR CLOUD. THERE'S DUST
EVERYWHERE AND YOUR MOTHERS AREN'T HERE TO
CLEAN IT UP FOR YOU.

GO TO IT! NOW! NOW! NOW! ON THE DOUBLE!

IRON PRODUCTION

In Which
Iron Is Produced in the Core of a
Massive Star, Resulting in Disaster

Once upon a time there were three stars, a little star (0.1 solar masses), a medium star (1 solar mass), and a big star (25 solar masses). All three were busy fusing hydrogen to helium, but because their masses were not the same, they each went about it in a different way.

The little star shone only as brightly as it thought wise, and used up its hydrogen fuel very slowly. Even though it had ten times less hydrogen than the medium star, it knew that its hydrogen would last 300 times longer (3 trillion years, in fact).

The medium star used up its hydrogen in 10 billion years and then started fusing helium to carbon and oxygen. But the helium only lasted a billion years, after which the medium star decided to be content with being a slowly cooling white dwarf.

But the big star was boastful and proud. "I'm more massive than my siblings; I will show them how brightly I can shine." Even though it had 25 times more hydrogen than the medium star, it used it up 1,400 times faster, and the hydrogen only lasted 7 million years. Then the big star started fusing helium to carbon, but that only lasted half a million years. In desperation, it started to fuse carbon to neon, which lasted only 600 years. After that it tried fusing neon (one year), oxygen (six months), and silicon (one day). It was left with a core of one and a half solar masses of iron at a temperature of 10 billion degrees Fahrenheit. And unfortunately for the big star, the protons and neutrons in iron nuclei are so tightly bound together that iron fusion doesn't produce energy, it requires energy instead. Now it felt as though 7 billion billion billion elephants were pressing down on its core, and the temperature rose even more until energetic photons completely disintegrated the iron nuclei. Within a fraction of a second, the core of the star imploded.

THE MORAL OF THE STORY:

The big star thought that 7 million years was a long time and that it didn't have to worry about such a distant future. After the hydrogen was gone, it realized that such wasteful energy production may not have been the wisest course of action, but it was too late to do anything about it.

26

SUPERNOVA EXPLOSION

In Which
a Massive Star Ends Its Life by Exploding

"Hum Parsec to Star Command, come in, Star Command. This is Hum Parsec reporting from the Milky Way Galaxy. My survey has just begun and I've found something interesting. Come in, Star Command!"

"This is Star Command, Parsec, we read you. What have you to report?"

"I've found a star that's about to explode, Star Command! According to my neutrino detector, silicon burning should be almost complete. There it goes, the core has collapsed! The density in the interior of the star is so high that electrons are combining with protons to make neutrons, releasing a billion billion billion billion billion billion neutrinos."

"Don't get cocky, Parsec! Even though individual neutrinos very rarely interact with matter, that many neutrinos could easily fry you. Remember, we need your report"

"Luckily for me, the density in the core is high enough that the neutrinos can't all escape immediately, so I'm safe for the moment. According to my measurements, the inner regions of the star are collapsing at almost 15% of the speed of light! They're about to hit the newly formed neutron star. Wow, what a shock wave! The material has rebounded and is flying away from the center of the star. It's going to take a few hours for the shock wave to reach the outer parts of the star, but meanwhile the high densities and neutrino fluxes are triggering fusion in the material and creating a whole host of elements heavier than iron."

"Get out of there fast, Parsec! That supernova will soon be more luminous than all the other stars in the Galaxy combined!"

"Roger that. I'm outta here!"

❑

"Come in, Star Command, this is Hum Parsec again. I am safely away from the supernova and am now able to report on the effects it is having on the surrounding area. Nearby clouds of hydrogen and helium gas are being compressed by the force of the explosion, and the heavy elements it created are being mixed with the clouds. Some of these clouds are now dense enough to become protostars, but the amount of metals is probably too small to create planets.

After a few more cycles of star formation and supernova explosions, however, this galaxy will almost certainly be full of stars with planetary systems."

"Make a full report of potential planetary systems and be sure to let us know if you find any that might be capable of supporting life. The Galaxy is depending on you, Hum Parsec!"

"Will do. Hum Parsec, signing off."

STAR FORMATION

In Which
the Sun Forms

> The following message is brought to you by GALSA, the
> Galactic Association of Licensed Stellar Agents.
> ❏
> "Because you don't want to trust your solar system to just any star."

"We're so glad we chose a GALSA star buyer's agent to find the right star for us. My husband and I wanted a star with a big enough habitable zone that we could have life on at least one planet, but we didn't have a lot of resources to spend. The buyer's agent showed us seven stars between 0.8 and 0.9 solar masses, but they just weren't right for us."

"Because they were looking in the 0.8 to 0.9 solar mass range, I knew that the surface temperature of these stars would be on the low side for their purposes. The stars would be emitting only 30 to 60 percent of the energy that a one solar mass star emits. But since they told me the mass range they'd be comfortable with, I had to trust that they knew what they wanted, so I only showed them stars in that mass range."

"The GALSA buyer's agent didn't put any pressure on us to increase our desired stellar mass range, even after we didn't find anything we liked.

But my husband and I talked it over and decided that we had the resources to go up to 1.0 solar masses, and that's what we told her."

"Once they raised their threshold to 1.0 solar masses, I had a much larger number of suitable stars that I could show them. They picked out five to examine in detail."

"The first three were just OK, and the fourth one my husband liked because it was in a good neighborhood, but I just fell in love with the fifth star we looked at. It was exactly 1.0 solar masses and there were nine planets forming around it, one of which was at a distance of 93 million miles from the star. Stars produce more energy with time, so the location of the habitable zone changes, but we calculated that this planet would be habitable for at least six billion years, by which time we will have long since retired. By then any life forms we decide to have should be big enough to take care of themselves."

"I'm glad that they were able to find a star that would make them happy, and I'm glad that I was able to help. I do a lot of big business throughout the Galaxy, but young couples finding their first star system always remind me of why I'm in the star system business in the first place."

"Since we were planning on having little ones we had the usual lead and radon inspections done. They found only 1 part per 10 billion of lead and no detectable radon in the star, which set our minds at ease. After getting a loan for the necessary resources, we signed the final papers and the star system was ours. And we owe it all to our GALSA buyer's agent!"

PLANETARY DIFFERENTIATION

In Which
the Planet Earth Forms

"Welcome back to 'The Planets Show' on the Galactic Value Channel. On the phone we have Marcia, who just bought P-21668, Jupiter. Hello, Marcia! How has your day been so far?"

"It's been great, just great, Tammi. How has your day been?"

"It's been wonderful. Tell me, Marcia, what made you decide to purchase Jupiter?"

"Well, I'll tell you, when I saw that it was forming in the outer solar system where the temperature is low and water could condense to form icy planetesimals, I knew that it would end up being massive enough to hold onto all its hydrogen and helium, and that it would be large enough to be a fantastic new fashion staple. Having so many moons was an added bonus for me. Also, I don't have a lot of time to wait for delivery, so the fact that it only takes about 10 million years to form was important to me."

"Well Marcia, it was great talking to you, and I'm sure you'll enjoy your new planet. Now it's time for today's special value, P-62164, the Earth, and it's safe to say it will not last. It's a terrestrial planet, which as you know is the number-one best-selling planetary type in our GVC collection.

"First, let me show you the width. As you can see, it comes in at just about 8000 miles. The Earth and the other terrestrial planets formed close to the sun out of kilometer-sized chunks of rocks. Because the temperature in the inner solar system was too high for ice to survive, the terrestrial planets had only about 10% of the planetesimals available to the outer planets, and therefore never got massive enough to hold onto hydrogen and helium. It will be a beautiful mixture of brown and blue, with about 70% of its surface covered by water. Isn't that wonderful? Just imagine relaxing in your very own ocean after a long, hard day. Big oceans like this are perfect for entertaining: you could have the whole Solar Neighborhood over!

"Oh my goodness, today's special value has just been sold!!! You know, when I saw that it was on the schedule I heard the writing on the wall and just knew it would go fast. Let's talk now with the buyer.

"Hi, Charlene, and welcome to 'The Planets Show.' How are you?"
"I'm just fine. How are you?"

"I'm doing great. Tell me, Charlene, why did you go for this planet?"

"Well, you know it's just so versatile, and when I saw that it was a special value I knew that I had to have it, even though it will take 100 million years to completely form. I was especially impressed by the way in which molten iron will percolate down through the silicate mantle to produce a spinning metallic core. I like my planets to have magnetic fields, you know, and that's one of the best ways to get one."

"It surely is. Charlene, tell us how you're going to use your new planet."

"Well, it just looks so terrific that I'm sure it's going to be a beautiful complement to my other planets. After the formation process is mostly complete, I'm expecting an atmosphere to form from the emission of volatile gases from volcanos, as well as from comet impacts. I might even decide to evolve some life down there."

"You know, Charlene, if you're looking to have life on your planet, then you might want to look into our giant moon option, which will help keep the tilt of the planet's spin axis constant and therefore provide a more stable environment for your organisms. Of course, it is a little bit more expensive, though."

"Why is that, Tammi?"

"In order to get such a large moon we would have to smash a protoplanet a few times more massive than Mars into the Earth. But I think the extra cost would be well worth it for you."

"That sounds just great. I'll definitely go for the giant moon option."

"Well thank you so much for shopping on GVC, Charlene, and enjoy your new planet!"

"Oh, I will, Tammi. Good-bye."

"Bye now. You take care.

VOLATILE GAS EXPULSION

In Which
the Atmosphere of the Earth is Produced

A forming planet:
Giant impacts destroy the
Early atmosphere.

      To the new planet,
      Asteroids and comets give
      volatile gases.

            Volcanoes emit
            Water, carbon dioxide,
            And other gases.

                  Ultraviolet light
                  Dissociates some water,
                  Making oxygen.

Carbon dioxide,
in excess, will heat the Earth.
Balance is needed.

        CO_2 disolves
        To form carbonic acid,
        H_2CO_3.

                H_2CO_3
                On rocks produces limestone,
                $CaCO_3$.

                        Subducted limestone
                        Feeds volcanoes that release
                        Carbon dioxide.

High temperatures mean
More evaporation and
Dissolved CO_2.

        As the CO_2
        Gets turned into limestone, the
        Temperature falls.

                Low temperatures mean
                Less evaporation and
                CO_2 builds up.

                        The CO_2 then
                        Acts to heat the atmosphere:
                        Rising temperatures.

The cycle goes on
For billions of years; watch as
The Sun gets brighter

A bright Sun means that
Less heating is needed: More
CO_2 in rocks.

On the early Earth
There was a thousand times more
Carbon dioxide.

Our atmosphere is
A very nice temperature.
Thank our friends the rocks.

♈

MOLECULAR REPRODUCTION

In Which
Life on Earth Begins

_____

Chapter 1

*

Night has 1,000 Chains

It was a dark and stormy night. In the shallow tide pool, a nucleic acid base collided with a sugar molecule. An amino acid sank beneath the murky depths. The tide pool had once been connected to the sea, but since then an army of sluggish days had marched by and evaporation had increased the concentration of organic molecules. Things had been tough for a long time but now it was easier for small chains of molecules to form. The air above the pool smelled of a rotten sweetness. A longer chain with a sinister look formed on the clay bottom, but then a speedy molecule slammed into it like brass knuckles on a Ming vase. It disappeared into the night.

Suddenly there was a bright flash of light and a giant explosion! A comet crashed nearby. In the upper atmosphere, water, methane, nitrogen, carbon dioxide, and hydrogen sulfide from the comet was shock-heated and converted into dozens of different organic molecules. They sped downward toward the tide pool. The shock wave from the impact hit the pool, increasing the temperature of the water like a match in a bathtub still. Short chains of molecules were knocked around like a washed-up boxer taking a dive.

When the Sun rose in the morning its bright ultraviolet light sped things up. Many complex chains of molecules were formed in the newly enriched pool. One of the new chains began to use the simpler molecules to reproduce itself. They began to feel like swimmers with concrete galoshes.

It didn't take long before most of the bit players were consumed and the tide pool was filled with copies of the new chain. Then a high tide came in and washed many of the big boys out to sea where they could begin to prey upon a new set of short, helpless chains of molecules. Other long chains continued to reproduce themselves in a shallow bay near the tide pool, feasting upon the small-frys in the neighborhood.

Many long chains lost their ability to make reproducing copies of themselves, but every so often a molecular chain formed that could reproduce itself even better than the rest, and soon the area was crawling with this kind of chain. Before long, the complex chains led to even *more* complicated groups of molecules. Today we call them bacteria.

Four billion years ago, they were the first life on Earth.

PROTEIN CONSTRUCTION

In Which
Proteins are Made from Amino Acids

> ## •WARNING•
> FAILURE TO FOLLOW THE ASSEMBLY INSTRUCTIONS IN THIS MANUAL MAY
> RESULT IN DEATH, DISEASE, OR OTHER SERIOUS INJURY TO YOU AND/OR TO
> NEIGHBORING ORGANISMS. USE CAUTION DURING ASSEMBLY AND USE. READ
> ALL INFORMATION CAREFULLY BEFORE STARTING ASSEMBLY.
> ## •WARNING•

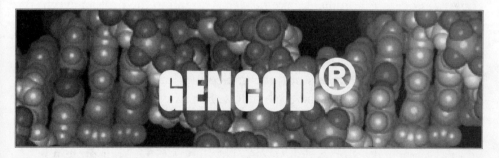

Thank you for purchasing a genetic code from GenCod, Inc. We at
GenCod are pleased to provide you with a genetic code that will allow
for a wide variety of design possibilities. With proper care, your genetic
code can last for billions of years or longer.

Your GenCod genetic code uses five nucleic acids*:

- ◆ adenine   (A)
- ◆ thymine   (T)
- ◆ guanine   (G)
- ◆ cytosine   (C)
- ◆ uracil   (U)

Adenine always bonds with thymine in DNA and with uracil in RNA. Thymine always bonds with adenine, guanine always bonds with cytosine, cytosine always bonds with guanine, and uracil always bonds with adenine.

DIRECTIONS:
1. To synthesize a protein, first partially uncoil the desired strand of DNA and produce a matching strand of RNA. For example, if your DNA strand begins with CGT, then your RNA strand will begin with GCA. After the copying process is complete, take the RNA strand to the protein synthesis site.

2. Once the RNA has been moved to the protein synthesis site, begin reading the strand in groups of three nucleotides each—codons—and adding amino acids using the table below. For example, if your RNA strand started with GGAAUCGUA, then you would begin your protein with glycine (GGA), isoleucine (AUC), and valine (GUA). Continue until you have reached a stop codon (UAA, UAG, or UGA). Your protein is now complete. Its function is determined by its three-dimensional structure, which is defined by the order of its amino acids.

*Please note that deoxyribonucleic acid (DNA) uses ATGC, while ribonucleic acid (RNA) uses AUGC, with uracil replacing thymine.

Your GenCod Genetic Code

Codon	Amino Acid	Codon	Amino Acid
UUU	phenylalanine	UCU	serine
UUC	phenylalanine	UCC	serine
UUA	leucine	UCA	serine
UUG	leucine	UCG	serine
CUU	leucine	CCU	proline
CUC	leucine	CCC	proline
CUA	leucine	CCA	proline
CUG	leucine	CCG	proline
AUU	isoleucine	ACU	threonine
AUC	isoleucine	ACC	threonine
AUA	isoleucine	ACA	threonine
AUG	methionine	ACG	threonine
GUU	valine	GCU	alanine
GUC	valine	GCC	alanine
GUA	valine	GCA	alanine
GUG	valine	GCG	alanine
UAU	tyrosine	UGU	cysteine
UAC	tyrosine	UGC	cysteine
UAA	stop	UGA	stop
UAG	stop	UGG	tryptophan
CAU	histidine	CGU	arginine
CAC	histidine	CGC	arginine
CAA	glutamine	CGA	arginine
CAG	glutamine	CGG	arginine
AAU	asparagine	AGU	serine
AAC	asparagine	AGC	serine
AAA	lysine	AGA	arginine
AAG	lysine	AGG	arginine
GAU	aspartic acid	GGU	glycine
GAC	aspartic acid	GGC	glycine
GAA	glutamic acid	GGA	glycine
GAG	glutamic acid	GGG	glycine

43

CAUTION: Your GenCod genetic code assumes that you will only be using left-handed (L-) amino acids. Mixing right-handed (D-) amino acids and left-handed amino acids will almost certainly result in misformed proteins and could cause death, disease, or other serious injury to you and/or to neighboring organisms. Refer to the diagram for pictures of L-alanine and D-alanine, the two stereoisomers of the amino acid alanine.

L-alanine   D-alanine

Your GenCod genetic code has been specially designed to be as error-free as possible—for example, if a mutation changed a GCA codon into a GCG codon then no change in the protein would occur since they both code for alanine. Despite the fact that your GenCod genetic code has been shown in laboratory tests to be more resilient to errors than 99.9999% of the possible genetic codes, some errors are inevitable and this should not be seen as a defect in our product. In fact, without such errors evolution would be impossible, and you would be unable to use the full power of your GenCod genetic code.

Thanks again for purchasing a genetic code from GenCod, Inc. We hope that it will provide you with billions of years of satisfactory use.

NOTE: These instructions for protein assembly using your GenCod genetic code will help insure that your protein synthesis goes smoothly and quickly. Be advised that any variation could result in unsatisfactory and/or dangerous proteins and a possible voiding of your warranty.

FERMENTATION

In Which
Bacteria Obtain Energy from their Surroundings

Polymers in the ocean get made
When organic compounds are sauteed
By lightning or heat,
Or a UV-light treat,
So that sugars like glucose pervade.

Early life on the Earth had to eat,
And glucose was a favorite treat.
Fermentation reduced
The glucose, and produced
Ethanol, CO2, and some heat.

"When there's lots of glucose that works fine,
But the levels are dropping with time.
If we made our own food,
It would really be shrewd—
Photosynthesis would be sublime."

"With CO2 and light in the mix,
I can make C6H12O6
And this glucose, you see,
Can be eaten by me,
So I'm no longer in such a fix."

CELL DIFFERENTIATION

In Which
Eukaryotic Life Arises

PROTEROZOIC FREE PRESS   June 6, 2,100,000,000 B.C.

PERSONALS—CALL 1-900-SYMBIOS

Are you interested in experimenting? Going beyond boring old symbiosis? Do you want to become part of your partner, or have your partner become part of you? If so, you've come to the right place to find the partner you've always dreamed of.

Hosts Seeking Endosymbionts	Endosymbionts Seeking Hosts
Recently nucleated cell seeks cyanobacterium to become chloroplast. I'll supply a protective environment with carbon dioxide, water, and access to light, you supply the chlorophyll, produce carbohydrates, and release oxygen. Together we can change the atmosphere! Ext. 1	Purple aerobic heterotroph wants to become a mitochondrion for a caring proteobacterium. I long to turn sugar and oxygen into energy, water, and carbon dioxide for you. Give me a call, you won't be disappointed! Ext. 3
If you can turn carbohydrates into energy then you've got what I need, baby. I can't wait to devour you! Ext. 2	Tired of doing everything yourself? Let me do the photosynthesis for you! I'll slip inside your cell walls and give you a lifetime of satisfaction. Ext. 4

RESPIRATION

In Which
Eukaryotes Evolve to Survive in an
Atmosphere with Increasing Amounts of Oxygen

FORAMINIFERA V 4.3

Enter DINOFLAGELLATE, DIPLOMONAD,
MICROSPORIDIAN, *and* TRICHOMONAD

20   FORAMY   If we are marked to die, we are enough
To do our Kingdom loss: and if to live,
The fewer organisms, the greater share of honor.
For in this era of increasing oxygen levels we must evolve,
And should we succeed then shall our names
Be as familiar as household words:
Dinoflagellate and Diplomonad,
Microsporidian, Trichomonad.°   *Eukaryotes*
This story shall all good eukaryotes teach their offspring:
And a geologic era shall never go by,
30   From this day to the ending of the world,
But we in it shall be remembered;
We few, we happy few, we band of protists,
For those today that change their metabolic processes with me
Shall be my siblings: be they never so vile,
This day shall gentle their condition.
And acritarchs° home a-bed   *Sleeping eukaryotes*
Shall think themselves accursed they were not here;
And hold their honor cheap, while any speaks
That evolved with us today.

47

MULTICELLULAR ORGANISMS

In Which
Organisms Composed of Multiple Cells Arise

ASSOCIATIVE DISORDERS
(or SINGLE PERSONALITY NEUROSES)

The essential feature of these disorders is the alteration of individual cells to become mutually dependent upon one another for various cellular functions. If it occurs with identical cells (as in Colonial Organism Disorder), then the cells become temporarily or permanently associated but little integration of cellular activities occurs. If the cells are not identical (as in Multicellular Organism Disorder), then cell specialization occurs to a lesser extent (as in Simple Multicellular Organism Disorder) or a greater one (as in Complex Multicellular Organism Disorder) extent.

314.15 Colonial Organism Disorder

The essential feature of this disorder is the existence of only one distinct state of being within a group of identical cellular organisms. A state of being is defined here as an enduring pattern of existence wherein the individual cells combine to participate in food consumption or production, reproduction, and locomotion as a single entity. In classic cases, the collection of cells is permanently associated as a colonial organism; in other cases, transient collections of cells can form a temporary aggregation.

Diagnostic criterion for 314.15 Colonial Organism Disorder
A. The existence of only one distinct state of being within a group of identical cellular organisms.

314.16 Multicellular Organism Disorder The essential feature of this disorder is the existence of one distinct state of being within a group of nonidentical cellular organisms. A state of being is defined here as an enduring pattern of existence wherein the individual cells combine to participate in food consumption or production, reproduction, and locomotion as a single entity. In classic cases (Complex Multicellular Organism Disorder), a large amount of cellular specialization occurs, with different types of cells being responsible for locomotion, reproduction, and other cellular functions. In other cases (Simple Multicellular Organism Disorder), only a limited amount of cellular specialization occurs.

Diagnostic criterion for 314.16 Multicellular Organism Disorder
A. The existence of only one distinct state of being within a group of non-identical cellular organisms.

SEXUAL REPRODUCTION

In Which
A New Form of Reproduction Occurs

TERRI! Show script
Air Date:
April 12, 700,000,000 B.C.
Rehearsal Date:
April 10, 700,000,000 B.C.

TERRI - HERE'S MONDAY'S SCRIPT. HAVE IT READY FOR REHEARSAL!

TERRI: Welcome to the **Terri! Show**. Boy, do we have a program for you today! I'm sure you've heard all about the hot new `lifestyle choice' that's just hit the unicellular community: 'protozoan chromosome swapping.' Today we have with us two pair of protozoans who have swapped chromosomes. We will protect their identities by calling them Protozoans 1,2,3 and 4.

[Zoom in on four protozoans sitting in chairs. Words appear at the bottom of the screen below each: PARTICIPATES IN CHROMOSOME SWAPPING.]

TERRI: Tell me Protozoan 1, why did you choose to swap chromosomes?

Protozoan 1: Well, Terri, it just feels so good to be able to exchange advantageous characteristics with loved ones. For example, if I develop a more efficient method of locomotion, I want my sweetheart to be able to move in the same way.

TERRI: Protozoan 2, can you tell me more about how chromosome swapping works?

Protozoan 2: When we're in the mood, my lover and I merge and share protoplasm, during which we do the chromosome swapping. Afterwards we separate and during our next cell division, our new chromosomes are used.

TERRI: That's fascinating. How about you number 3, where do you imagine this leading?

Protozoan 3: Terri, I want to be able to join with my partners more intimately by giving them all of my chromosomes while keeping copies for myself. Then we'll all be able to use the best genetic ideas.

TERRI: I see. Protozoan 4, do you have anything to add?

Protozoan 4: Yes, Terri, I do. I agree with what 3 has to say, but I foresee an even greater advance, in which instead of reproducing by dividing into two identical cells, we divide into four cells, each containing half of our genetic information. These cells would then be able to join with cells from other protozoans, and we would have a very efficient method of producing new traits, which could then be tested via natural selection. I call it sexual reproduction and I think that everyone will be doing it soon.

TERRI: We have a question from the audience.

First audience plant: Don't you really think that all this is a completely disgusting perversion of nature?

Second audience plant: It's worse than those perverts from last week who were picking up whatever genetic material they happened to find floating around!

First audience plant, again: Yeah, that's disgusting!!

Other audience plants: Get them off the stage!! I'm not letting my daughter cells listen to such filth!!!

[Audience plants begin to rush the stage and start to fight. Terri, you'll pretend to try to calm everyone down. There will be screaming and shouting, and the camera will shake back and forth, before it goes dark.]

527 Million years B.C.   **The Earth**

EVOLUTIONARY DIVERSIFICATION

In Which
the Diversity of Life Forms on Earth
Increases Greatly in a Relatively Short Time

INTERNAL MEMORANDUM

TO: Staff   **FR:** Dr.Palaeolyngbya

RE: R.A.A.C. press   **DATE:** 3/20/527,000,000 B.C

See the attached article from <u>Deep Time</u> magazine.
Terrific coverage of the program--we should all be
proud of ourselves!

54

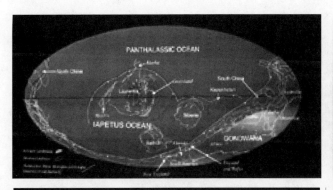

WORLD

Space exploration is off to a roaring start.

Eric Schulman reports from the Iapetus Ocean

Bacterial scientists announced today that the first stage of a 500-million-year space program had been successfully completed. The head of the project, Dr. Palaeolyngbya, reported the results at the annual meeting of the RAAC, the Rodinia Association for the Advancement of Cyanobacteria. Bacterial astronomers recently discovered that in only six billion years the sun will run out of hydrogen in the core and expand to engulf the Earth.

Dr. Palaeolyngbya's team is responsible for developing the capability to explore the solar system and the Galaxy for new places to live. "When we started this project fifteen million years ago," explained Dr. Palaeolyngbya, "we hoped to be able to develop simple multicellular organisms that would then evolve into life forms that we could use in order to explore the Galaxy. The results have exceeded our wildest dreams." Another member of the team, Dr. Langiella, noted, "It only took about three million years for us to develop a wide variety of animals, including sponges, mollusks, brachiopods, segmented as well as nonsegmented worms, arthropods, echinoderms, and chordates."

"We're off to a great start, but the next part of the project will take a much longer time," pointed out Dr. Gloeocapsomorpha. Dr. Gloeocapsomorpha is leading the effort to evolve the arthropods into "intelligent" creatures that will be able to build space ships to leave the Earth, taking bacteria volunteers with them. "Because most arthropods are protected by chitinous shells. they should be very well prepared for the dangerous tasks ahead of them," pointed out Dr. Gloeocapsomorpha.

Although the arthropods appear to have the best chance to complete the project, a small group is trying to evolve the chordates. "It's never a good idea to depend on just one kind of organism," pointed out Dr. Kidstoniella, who leads the group. "That's why we decided to develop so many at the start. For example, my chordates appear to have the potential to develop quite a sophisticated nervous system if they manage to survive long enough."

The bacterial scientists estimate that it will take about half a billion years to develop the capability for space flight, and then another few hundred million years to completely colonize the Galaxy. "We should have plenty of time," Dr. Palaeolyngbya said at the conclusion of the meeting, "but it's always better to be safe than sorry."

TRILOBITE DOMINATION

In Which
Trilobites Rule the Earth

Two million score and seven years ago our ancestors brought forth upon this planet a new subphylum: conceived in the Cambrian, and dedicated to the proposition that all arthropods are not created equal.

Now we are testing whether this subphylum, or any subphylum so conceived and so dedicated, can long endure. We are met here on a great battlefield of the struggle. We have come to dedicate a portion of it as a final resting place for those who here gave their lives that this subphylum might live. It is altogether fitting and proper that we should do this.

But, in a larger sense we can not dedicate —we can not consecrate —we can not hallow this mud. The brave trilobites, living and dead, who struggled here have consecrated it, far above our poor power to add or detract. The world will little note, nor long remember, what we say here, but it can never forget what they did here. It is for us the living, rather, to be dedicated here to the unfinished work that they who fought here have thus far so nobly advanced. It is rather for us to be here dedicated to the great task remaining before us — that from these honored dead we take increased devotion to that cause for which they gave the last full measure of devotion — that we here highly resolve that these dead shall not have died in vain; that this subphylum, under water, shall dominate the oceans; and that those species with compound eyes, with three lobes, and with numerous delicate legs shall not perish from this Earth (for at least another 250 million years).

Land Exploration

In which
Animals First Venture onto Land

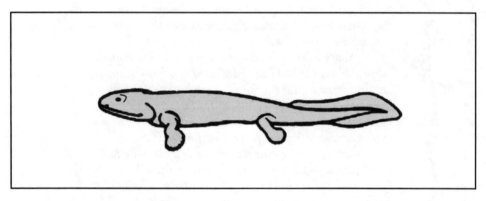

Dr. A. gunnari, P.I.

COVER SHEET FOR PROPOSAL TO THE TETRAPOD SCIENCE FOUNDATION

PROGRAM ANNOUNCEMENT/SOLICITATION NO.	FOR TSF USE ONLY
	TSF PROPOSAL NUMBER
FOR CONSIDERATION BY TSF UNIT(S)	

DATE RECEIVED	COPIES	DIVISION ASSIGNED	FUND CODE	FILE LOCATION

TITLE OF PROPOSED PROJECT: Colonization of Land (COL)

PRINCIPAL INVESTIGATOR: Acanthostega gunnari

PROPOSED DURATION: 35 Million years

CHECK BOXES IF THIS PROPOSAL INCLUDES ANY OF THE ITEMS LISTED BELOW:

BEGINNING INVESTIGATOR ☐	DISCLOSURE OF LOBBYING ACTIVITIES ☐
ENVIRONMENTAL POLICY ☐	PROPRIETARY OR PRIVILEGED INFORMATION ☐
VERTEBRATE ANIMALS ☒	LARGE GRANT FOR EXPLORATORY RESEARCH ☒

ABSTRACT:

Over 25% of the surface of the planet is covered by land, an untapped resource that has been used very little to date due to the lack of adaptations to a non-water environment. In research funded by a previous TSF grant, we developed lungs to extract oxygen from air in addition to the oxygen we get from the water with gills. These lungs have since been used extensively in shallow stagnant ponds and bays where the oxygen content in the water is too low for gills to function properly. In the present proposal we are requesting funds to support the development of strong limb bones and flexible joints so that we will be able to begin the colonization of land (COL).

Successful COL requires that we deal with new physical problems. For example, because air is much less dense than water, on land the downward gravitational force will not be balanced by an upward buoyancy force. We will therefore need compact and muscular bodies to overcome the force of gravity.

For complete COL we will need to be able to reproduce out of the water. This will require eggs that will hold water while being permeable to the oxygen that is so important to developing embryos. Although this problem is difficult, it is not intractable, and it will be the subject of a future TSF grant proposal if the current proposal is funded and successful.

Signatures
_____

_____
Acanthostega gunnari, P.I.

_____
YIchthyostega, Co-I.

_____
Metaxygnathus, Dean

By signing and submitting this proposal, the applicant is certifying that the statements herein (excluding scientific hypotheses and scientific opinions) are true and complete, and is hereby providing certifications regarding debt status, debarment and suspension, drug-free workplace, and lobbying activities, as set forth in the TSF Grant Proposal Guide.

COMET COLLISION

In Which
a Comet Hits the Earth

Once upon a time, on a warm June day about 65 million years ago, while Shelley Shrew was sleeping under a big green leaf on an island near the Yucatan peninsula in what is now Mexico, a comet hit her on the head, killing her instantly. The comet—or perhaps an asteroid—was 10 miles across and hit Shelley with a velocity of about 50,000 miles per hour, creating a crater 100 miles wide and releasing an amount of energy equivalent to 100 million megatons of TNT, which is 1000 times more powerful than all the currently existing nuclear weapons combined. The impact produced at least six tsunamis, some of which were more than 300 feet high, a magnitude 12 earthquake, a deluge of sulfuric acid rain, an enormous amount of carbon dioxide released into the atmosphere that increased the average global temperature by 20 degrees Fahrenheit for a million years, a global firestorm that incinerated about 25% of the living biomass, and a huge cloud of dust that blocked the light from the Sun for months and contributed to the extinction of nearly every land animal whose adult form weighed more than about 50 pounds, including the dinosaurs.

All in all, it was a bad day for Shelley and not a particularly good day for the Earth, either.

DINOSAUR EXTINCTION

In Which
the Dinosaurs Die

_____

I've lost you, you've lost me,
We're as dead as dead can be.
'Cause a 10-mile comet
    smashed into the Earth,
There won't be more dino births.

I've lost you, you've lost me,
We're now part of history.
But descendants of shrews
    will worship you and me,
We'll be stars of kids' TV.

MAMMAL EXPANSION

In Which
Many Species of Mammals Develop

MAMMALIA CLASS PROSPECTUS
A Balanced Class of Vertebrates

TAM-CO, Tertiary Animal Management Company (formerly Cretaceous Animal Management, Inc.)
Pangea, Earth

The Mammalia Class is a diversified open-ended class of vertebrates that seeks to provide long-term growth. The Class invests about 65% of its species in placental mammals, about 32% of its species in marsupial mammals, about 3% in multituberculates, and less than 0.1% in monotremes.*

CLASS INCEPTION DATE: 225 Million years B.C.

SUBCLASSES (4):

*The Class's species are NOT guaranteed or insured by any government agency. As with any investment that is subject to wide fluctuations in environmental conditions, you could lose resources by investing in the Class. These species have not been approved or disapproved by the Species and Environmental Commission, nor has the Species and Environmental Commission passed upon the accuracy or adequacy of this prospectus. Any representation to the contrary is a criminal offense. Remember that past performance is not necessarily indicative of future returns.

1. Monotremes: The original mammals that evolved from reptiles about 225 million years B.C., monotremes have become much less common with time. Examples include the spiny anteater and the platypus.

2. Multituberculates: These mammals have many cusps on their teeth. Although they have been fairly successful in the past, there are signs that they may become extinct by about 20 million years B.C. Examples include the prairie-dog-like Lambdopsalis and the squirrel-like Ptilodus.

3. Marsupials: A highly successful subclass, especially in some parts of the world, marsupials have short gestational periods. The offspring complete their development in the mother's pouch. Examples include the possum and kangaroo.

4. Eutheria: The Eutheria are placental mammals and are the most successful mammal subclass, with indications that they will become even more successful over time. Placental mammals bear live young that are nourished before birth by a placenta. Examples include the tapir and the shrew.

INVESTMENT STRATEGY: The Class invests in species that show great promise for future returns. As a result of the failure of the Dinosauria subclass in 65 million years B.C., the Mammalia Class has shown a great deal of recent diversification, especially among the carnivorous mammals.**

**The current strategy of heavy investment in carnivorous mammals is not fundamental and can therefore be changed without shareholder approval provided shareholders are given 3 million years notice.

HOMO SAPIENS MANIFESTATION

In Which
Modern Human Beings Appear

Welcome to the neighborhood!

Has your species just evolved? If so, we're here to help. One of our cheerful representatives will be very glad to bring you a basket full of useful information and free gifts. We'll also be happy to answer any questions and provide you with any information you may require to address your changing needs.

Feeling out of place?

Are you used to an arboreal way of life? You needn't feel alienated, even so. Those flexible digits and forward-facing eyes can also be very useful on the savannah. Let us show you how in a warm, friendly, and professional way.

Disconnected?

You diverged from monkeys about twenty million years ago and from chimps about five million years ago, so you're probably feeling a bit disconnected from your roots. We understand what you're going through, and you can count on us to be there for you.

A little slow on your feet?

Even though you've been bipedal for three million years, it still takes some getting use to, doesn't it? Just remember, walking has freed your hands for carrying, tool use, and accepting our free gifts.

Don't worry—you have what it takes to make it!

Your brain has been getting bigger for the past two million years, so you're now smart enough to realize what a great deal this service is and to understand the advertisements that we'll include in your basket for free.

EDS. A name you can trust.

At Evolutionary Development Services, we've been bringing together different species in a spirit of cooperation for millions of years. With our service, everyone is a winner!

LANGUAGE ACQUISITION

In Which
Human Beings Develop Spoken Language

> OG: "Grunt grunt grunt grunt grunt grunt, Thagg."
> THAGG: "Og!, Grunt grunt grunt grunt?"
> OG: "Grunt Thagg grunt Og grunt!"
> THAGG: "Grunt."

What are Thagg and Og doing? They are TALKING, and you too can exchange information orally after you take this simple course in spoken language.

1. Let's take a look at the sounds of spoken language.

Consonants	Vowels
g as in *grunt*.	**u** as in *grunt*
r as in *grunt*	
n as in *grunt*	
t as in *grunt*	

2. Note that the syllable can be stressed or unstressed, depending on whether the speaker wishes to emphasize what he or she is saying.

Below are the parts of speech used in spoken language.

Simple nouns	Compound nouns
grunt, *water*	**grunt grunt,** *water buffalo*
grunt, *buffalo*	**grunt grunt,** *buffalo water*

Verbs	Pronouns
grunt, *do*	**grunt,** *I*
grunt, *eat*	**grunt,** *you*

Adverbs	Conjunctions
grunt, *quickly*	**grunt**, *and*
grunt, *slowly*	**grunt**, *but*

Adjectives	Articles
grunt, *yellow*	**grunt**, *the*
grunt, *brown*	**grunt**, *a*

3. Syntax in spoken language is relatively straightforward. The basic sentence structure is Subject-Verb-Object:

<u>Basic sentences</u>

Grunt grunt grunt.

I eat buffalo.

Grunt grunt grunt.

You drink water.

<u>Compound sentence</u>

Grunt grunt grunt grunt grunt grunt grunt.

You drink water and I eat buffalo.

<u>Complex sentence</u>

Grunt grunt grunt grunt grunt grunt grunt grunt grunt grunt grunt grunt grunt, Thagg.

Eat the brown water buffalo but do not drink the yellow buffalo water, Thagg.

4. Once you've mastered simple spoken language, you'll be able to learn advanced spoken language and express complicated ideas such as the following:

Thagg, grunt grunt grunt grunt grunt grunt grunt grunt grunt grunt grunt grunt grunt grunt grunt grunt grunt, grunt grunt grunt grunt grunt grunt grunt grunt grunt grunt grunt grunt grunt, grunt grunt grunt grunt grunt grunt grunt grunt grunt, grunt.

Thagg, it occurs to me that if you hold the stone you wish to flake in one hand, and the stone with which you intend to strike it in the other, after which you strike the one with the other, then you may obtain much more efficacious tools than if you continue using your current method of throwing the second stone at the first while it is laying on the ground.

GLACIATION

In Which
A Thousand-Year Ice Age Begins

"And in other news, Mount Toba on the island of Sumatra erupted today, putting 200 cubic miles of ash into the atmosphere. It was the largest volcanic eruption in over 400 million years. Wow. Now it's time for the weather with our weatherman Dr. Dan."

"Thanks, Lisa! Let's have a quick look at the weather map.

"The forecast for tonight is dark. Darkness will continue for the next several weeks as ash from the volcano covers about 20% of the planet, and temperatures will begin to drop. The temperature will be about 20 degrees lower than average for the next six years, and I'm forecasting that approximately three-quarters of all plants in the Northern Hemisphere won't survive. In addition, global snow cover will reflect much of the Sun's light, causing a world-wide ice age that will last a thousand years and kill off all but a few thousand people. Back to you, Lisa."

"Thanks, Dr. Dan! Now let's see how this global catastrophe is likely to affect our local sports teams. . . ."

INNOVATION

In Which
Advanced Tools Are Widely Used

ARE YOU STILL USING STONE TOOLS?

Of course you are. who isn't? After all, stone tools are reliable. You can trust them. They've been around for hundreds of thousands of years. BUT . . .

HAVE YOU THOUGHT ABOUT WHAT BONE TOOLS COULD DO FOR YOU?

That's right, BONE TOOLS. Bone Is durable, but much easier to work with than stone. Your parents mostly scavenged, but if you want to hunt, then BONE TOOLS are right for you! Use Bone to make deadly spear heads and harpoon tips.

SPEARS WITH STONE ARE OK, BUT SPEARS WITH BONE GO ALL THE WAY!

But don't throw those stone tools away: Use them to make BONE TOOLS! Flint chisels can be used to make great spear heads out of antlers. Flint scrapers are very helpful in shaping Bone and in processing hides. And think about all the things that can be done with FLINT BLADES.

73

BONE TOOLS AND FLINT BLADES HAVE PROVEN RELIABILITY!

Some folks have been using Blades on and off for more than two hundred thousand years, and BONE TOOLS go back almost that far. Now's the time to switch, because BONE TOOLS and FLINT BLADES will satisfy the demands of your new lifestyle! Don't just use the same old stone tools your parents used.

THINK NEW. THINK BOLD. THINK BONE.

Paid for by the Aurignacian Bone Tool Advisory Council.

RELIGION

In Which
a Diversity of Beliefs Arise

Ceremonialism. Shamanism. Paganism. Occultism. Mysticism. Pantheism. Polytheism. Hinduism. Judaism. Mithraism. Druidism. Zoroastrianism. Buddhism. Confucianism. Taoism. Atheism. Jainism. Skepticism. Shinto. Transcendentalism. Stoicism. Catholicism. Manichaeism. Agnosticism. Neoplatonism. Islam. Sufism. Scholasticism. Sikhism. Lutheranism. Anabaptists. Mennonites. Anglicans. Calvinism. Macumba. Humanism. Deism. Presbyterianism. Baptists. Quakers. Amish. Freemasonry. Hasidism. Methodism. Spiritualism. Martinism. Shakers. Santeria. Episcopalians. Mormonism. Tenrikyo. Babism. Christadelphianism. Oneida. Spiritism. Baha'i. Seventh Day Adventists. Jehovah's Witnesses. Theosophy. Christian Science. Pentecostalism. Integral Yoga. Serpent Handlers. Gurdjieff. Assemblies of God. Rosicrucian Order. Bruderhof. Fundamental-ism. Branch Davidians. Seicho-No-Ie. Rastafarianism. Shirdi Sai Baba. Branhamism. Urantia. Neo-Paganism. Scientology. Unification Church. Ananda Marga Yoga. Transcendental Meditation. Discordianism. Synanon Church. Unitarian Universal-ism. NeoPentecostalism. Sri Chinmoy. Eckankar. Satanism. Christian Reconstructionism. Suma Ching Hai. Aum Shinrikyo. Chen Tao. Kibology. Scientific Pantheism.

ANIMAL DOMESTICATION

In Which
Humans Domesticate Animals

"Hi, Rex. Long time no see."

"Mornin,' Spot. You look well-rested. What's new with you?"

"Me and my pack bought a tribe of humans from Rover last month. Best hundred bones we ever spent! They do most of the work taking down the prey and I get as much as I can eat. Plus this fire stuff they have keeps me nice and warm at night. And they keep the big predators away. It's a sweet setup."

"How did Rover manage to domesticate them?"

"Didn't you know? His pack has been raising humans for years and years now. Every generation the humans get better and better trained. One of these days we won't have to do any hunting at all! We'll snooze in the sun all day and they'll bring food to us whenever we want. You should get yourself a tribe."

"I don't know, it sounds pretty boring to me."

"Suit yourself. I, for one, don't mind not work-ing. Say hi to your pack for me, Rex."

"Take care, Spot."

FOOD SURPLUS PRODUCTION

In Which
Humans Develop Agriculture

"I'm hungry. I haven't been able to find any roots or berries today and the guys are out chasing cheetahs or something."

"They never learn, do they? How many times do I have to tell them not to go after fast food. They'll never—hey, are you all right?"

"Oooh, my head. The moment you said `fast food' I felt like I was someone else, two hundred thousand moons from now, in a place called Pittsburgh, and that I had just invented a new kind of food."

"A new kind of food? Do you think we could find some around here?"

"I'm not even sure I know what kind of food it was. Apparently, it was composed of two patties of beef, a special kind of sauce, and lettuce, cheese, pickles, and onions, all of which were on a bun that had sesame seeds on it. Whatever that all means."

"What are you talking about? The only thing I understood was 'seed.' Hey, I wonder whether we could eat the seeds of any of the grasses that grow around here."

"What—you mean all this wheat, barley, oats, and millet? The thought never occurred to me, but it's worth a try! We could probably boil them, beat them, mix them with water, shape them into loaves, bake them, and serve them with some of that gooey goat milk that we left out in the sun too long."

"Hmm . . . I don't think that's exactly what you meant by all those strange words, but it is a start. Have you thought about what to name your new food?"

"Yes, I'm going to call it 'bread and cheese.' If we like it, then maybe we can figure out some way of growing more grain so that there will always be plenty to go around!"

INSCRIPTION

In Which
Writing is Invented

The Sumerian History of the Universe in 30 Words or Less:

Lakhmu and Lakhamu incarnation ... Anshar and Kishar creation ... Enki and Ninki assignation ... Marduk maturation ... Tiamat confrontation ... Heaven and Earth production ... People construction ... Animal domestication ... Food surplus production ... Inscription ... Composition ... Extrapolation?

WARRING NATIONS

In Which
Nation Battles Nation for Resources

_____

50 WAYS TO LOOT YOUR NEIGHBOR

The problem is too much discontent
She said to me
The answer is easy if you
Take it logically.
I'd like to help you do your duty
As marquis,
There must be fifty ways
To loot your neighbor

She said, It's really not my habit
To intrude
Furthermore I hope my meaning
Won't be lost or misconstrued
So I repeat myself, at the risk of being crude
There must be fifty ways to loot your neighbor
Fifty ways to loot your neighbor

CHORUS:
Just put on your belt, Celt
Make off with the loot, Jute

Set fire to the cot, Scot
Then bring back the gold
Go kill and maim, Dane
Stop being humane
Hurt, wound, and stun, Hun
Take all you can hold

She said it shocks me so
To hear that you will not expand
And I wish that you would reconsider
Following my plan
I said I appreciate that
But I'll have no more talk
About the fifty ways

She said if that's your final
Word I'll acquiesce
Furthermore there is a plan
That I like better, I confess
And then she killed me
Took my land, and became marquise
There must be fifty ways
To loot your neighbor
Fifty ways to loot your neighbor

CHORUS

EMPIRE CREATION AND DESTRUCTION

In Which
the First Empire in Human History Comes and Goes

DUMMM-DA-DUM-DUM. DUMMM-DA-DUM-DUM-DUMM!

THE STORY YOU ARE ABOUT TO READ IS TRUE. ONLY THE UNIVERSITY HAS BEEN
CHANGED TO PROTECT OUR FUNDING.

JOE [voice-over]: This is the desert. Also called the Fertile Crescent.
Today there's nothing but sand as far as the eye can see. But underneath
the sand lies evidence of ancient civilizations. That's where I come in.
I'm an archaeologist. I carry a shovel.

DUM-DA-DUMM. DUM-DA-DUM-DA-DUMM.
DUM-DA-DUMM. DUM-DA-DUM-DA-DUMM.

JOE [voice-over]: It was Monday, March 13th, 9:05 a.m. I was working off a National Science Foundation grant through the University of Michigan. The chair of the department is Professor Kelly. My partner is Dr. Frank Gannon. My name's Friday.

JOE: How was your weekend, Frank?

FRANK: Pretty good, Joe. I spent most of it watching basketball.
[The phone rings.]

JOE [answering]: Archaeology, Friday. Yeah. Uh-huh. Um-hum. Hm . . . Is that right? Yeah. Um-hum. Uh-huh. OK. We'll get right on it.

FRANK: What's the matter, Joe?

JOE: We've got a 203 on our hands, Frank.

FRANK: You mean an unexplained disappearance of the Akkadian Empire, formed by Sargon in 2370 B.C., which at its peak stretched 800 miles from the Persian Gulf to the headwaters of the Euphrates River in present-day Turkey?

JOE: Yeah. That's the one.

FRANK: Hard to believe. It was the world's first empire and it ended for no apparent reason.

JOE: Let's go check it out.

DUM-DA-DUMM. DUM-DA-DUM-DA-DUMM.
DUM-DA-DUMM. DUM-DA-DUM-DA-DUMM.

JOE [voice-over]: 7:17 a.m. After flying to the Habur Plains in Syria, we spoke to a Dr. Glassner.

GLASSNER: Ah yes, the Akkadian Empire. For 100 years between 2300 B.C. and 2200 B.C., Akkadian governors ruled cities all over the Fertile Crescent. Caravans of hundreds of donkeys traveled 12 hours a day or more to and from Armenia, and ships full of timber sailed to Egypt and returned with fish, flax, papyrus, alabaster, lentils, and gold.

JOE: And then what happened?

GLASSNER: No one knows, Dr. Friday.

FRANK: Surely there are theories.

GLASSNER: Oh, the usual. Overreaching leaders, faltering armies, overuse of farmland, but none of them really fit.

JOE: Mind if we look around?

GLASSNER: Not at all, be my guest.

DUM-DA-DUMM, DUM-DA-DUM-DA-DUMM.

JOE [voice-over]: 4:21 p.m. After spending 12 years in field research, Frank and I get together to compare notes.

84

JOE: What have you found?

FRANK: It looks like the population in the north abandoned their homes and moved south into the cities, overtaxing water and food supplies and leading to urban chaos. But I still don't understand why.

JOE: Take a look at these northern soil samples for the period between 2300 and 2200 B.C.

FRANK: Everything looks fine.

JOE: Now take a look at these soil samples from the following 300 years.

FRANK: Hmm . . . this soil has very few earthworm holes but lots of wind-blown fine dust. It must have had almost no water in it. If the north dried out, then the wheat, barley, and sheep that provided the empire with wealth would have disappeared. Of course! Climate change destroyed the Akkadian Empire. Should've been obvious from the start.

DUM-DA-DUMM. DUM-DA-DUM-DA-DUMM.
DUM-DA-DUMM. DUM-DA-DUM-DA-DUMM.

The story you have just read is true. Only the university has been changed to protect our funding.

Upon arrival back in Ann Arbor, Friday and Jones wrote up their results and submitted a series of papers to the American Journal of Archaeology.

Explaining the disappearance of the Akkadian Empire is rewardable by not less than tenure and not more than promotion to full professor.

DUM-DA-DUMM. DUM-DA-DUM-DA-DUMM . . .

CIVILIZATION

In Which
Many and Sundry Events Occur

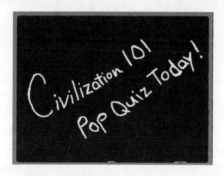

"Good morning class, and welcome back to Civilization 101. I hope that you studied your textbook well over break because we're having an oral pop quiz today on. . . let's see, how about years ending in 17 since 1700 B.C.? OK, David, what happened in 917 B.C.?"

"Um . . . King Rehoboam I of Judah died? He was the son of King Solomon and because of his misrule the northern tribes broke away from Jerusalem and established the kingdom of Israel. For some reason the northern tribes didn't particularly want to be 'scourged with scorpions' by Rehoboam (1 Kings 12:14)."

"Indeed. Melissa, what happened in 217 B.C.?"

"Let's see, that was during the Second Punic War. Wasn't that the year Hannibal defeated the main Roman army at Lake Trasimeno? By this time all his elephants had perished, and despite his military victories, his home of Carthage failed to give him sufficient support. In the end, he could never muster enough strength to assault Rome itself in the fifteen years that his army ravaged Italy. He might have done better had he brought extra warm-weather gear for the elephants."

"They do get cold in the snow, don't they? Elizabeth, what happened in 517 A.D.?"

"517. Yes, that was when Emperor Wu-Ti became a Buddhist and introduced Buddhism to central China. Shortly thereafter he met the first Patriarch of Zen Buddhism. When asked by the emperor, 'What is the essence of Buddhism?', the Zen Master replied, 'No essence whatsoever.'"

"That pretty much says it all. Andrew, how about 1417 A.D.?"

"That was when the Council of Constance elected Pope Martin V, ending the Great Schism. In 1378 the cardinals had elected Urban VI as Pope, but within four months they had declared that election null and void and elected Clement VII instead, creating two lines of Popes. By 1409, after three new Popes in one line and one new Pope in the other, the Popes were Gregory XII and Benedict XIII. The Council of Pisa then met and declared Alexander V to be Pope. He soon died and was replaced by John

XXIII, but Gregory XII and Benedict XIII refused to step down, so now there were three Popes. It wasn't until the Council of Constance that Gregory XII resigned and the other two Popes were deposed."

"Forty years is certainly a long time to have a plethora of Popes. Shelley, can you tell me what happened in 1517 A.D.?"

"Of course. That was the year Martin Luther felt compelled to protest the Church's granting of indulgences. He nailed his 95 theses to the church door in Wittenberg and started down the path that would lead to the Protestant Reformation and eventually to Garrison Keillor."

"Indeed. Dale, 1717 A.D.?"

"1717? Um . . . 1717? Oh, yeah, that was the year that Yoshimune became the eighth shogun of the Tokugawa Shogunate. Only 33 when he became shogun, he was known as one of the wisest rulers in the history of Japan. He carried out many reforms and encouraged the martial arts and education. Right?"

"I'm sorry, Dale. Your facts about Yoshimune are correct, but he became shogun in 1716, not in 1717. How many times do I have to tell you to read the text before class? Try to do better next time. Ah, I see that class is about over for today. Tomorrow we're going to be discussing the pre-amble to the Constitution of the United States. Please try to read it tonight. OK, Dale?"

CONSTITUTION

In Which
a Constitution is Written

FAST DOCUMENTS

CONSTITUTION HUT

"Constitutions with all the toppings!"
Fast, revolutionary service.
Tax-free delivery
Call 4-P E O P L E —24 hrs.

Rrrrrrriing...

—Thank you for calling Constitution Hut, can you hold please?... Thanks for waiting. Can I take your order?

—OK, that's one constitution to be delivered to General— sorry, *Mr.* Washington and the Philadelphia convention to revise the Articles of Confederation.

—What would your convention like in the constitution, Mr. Washington? Bicameral legislature, sure, we can do that. Direct election of the House of Representatives, OK. Senators chosen by the state legislatures, mm-hmm—sure you don't want direct election of senators? OK, OK, never mind.

—What else? The executive branch will be headed by a president, whose term will be four years. President and vice-president to be elected by electors from each state, chosen in a fashion approved by the state legislature. You're sure about that electors idea?

—Fine. The president will be the person who receives the most electoral votes, and the vice-president will be the person who receives the second-largest number of electoral votes. Now this really seems like a bad idea to me. What if they have completely opposing views on important issues? What if . . .

—OK, OK, I know you could've chosen to call Constitution King. Yes, I know their advertising says that special orders don't upset them. Oh, very well, what else? Judicial power to the Supreme Court, OK. New states admitted to the union by Congress, right. Constitution can be amended by Congress and the states. Good idea, that.

—What else? No religious test shall ever be required as a qualification to any office or public trust, OK. Nine states required to ratify. Will that be all? Sure you don't want any extra rights in there? Well, give us a call if you change your mind.

—OK, we'll fill in the details and get this to you by September 17. Thank you for choosing Constitution Hut.

INDUSTRIALIZATION

In Which
Automated Manufacturing
and Agriculture Revolutionize the World

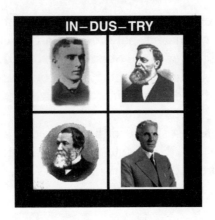

When you found yourself with too few farm hands,
Cy McCormick came to you
Speaking words of wisdom: industry.
When you needed uniforms,
Isaac Singer showed you what to do:
Use his sewing machine: industry.
Industry, industry,
Industry, industry.
Lots of new inventions: industry.

After Hargreaves' spinning jenny came
And we had the factory,
Arkwright knew the answer: Industry.
For though the Luddites break looms there is
Still a chance that they will see
They can all get jobs in industry.
Industry, industry,
Industry, yeah, industry.
They can all get jobs in industry.

When Richard Sears figured out
Conveyor belts for assembly,
One more step down the path: Industry.
Then Henry Ford studied the process,
And he made the model T.
Motorcars for workers: Industry.
Industry, industry,
Industry, industry.
Lots of new inventions: industry.
Industry, industry,
Industry, yeah, industry.
They can all get jobs in industry.

Words & Music by Schulman and Schulman
(with apologies to Paul McCartney)

93

WORLD CONFLAGRATIONS

In Which
Most of the World Is at War

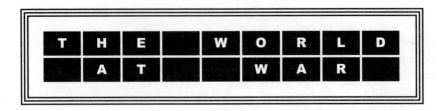

"Good evening, and welcome to 'The World at War,' the game show that lets *you* decide the fate of the world. Our first contestant is Colonel Dragutin Dimitrijevic from Serbia. Colonel Dimitrijevic, it's June of 1914 and you want to insure Serbia's independence from Austria-Hungary. What should you do?"

"Give weapons to Bosnian youths who intend to assassinate Austro-Hungarian Archduke Ferdinand in Sarajevo?" [buzzer]

"No, I'm sorry, that would result in Austria, Germany, and Bulgaria declaring war on Serbia, the defeat of the Serbian army, and the incorporation of Serbia into Yugoslavia after World War I.

"Next up we have Count Alfred von Schlieffen of Germany. Count von

Schlieffen, what should Germany do when faced with the prospect of war with both Russia and France?"

"Bypass the French armies by attacking through neutral Belgium, crushing enemy's flanks, and completing the destruction by attack from the rear. France will be defeated in 39 days, before Russia has a chance to mobilize!" [buzzer]

"A good try, but French and British armies would be able to retreat in good order, to counterattack near the Marne River, and to establish a firm defense. In addition, this plan would require Germany to attack France as soon as Russia mobilized, regardless of whether it was a strategically good time to do so.

"Now we have Prime Minister Salandra of Italy. Prime Minister, the Great War has started and Italy has declared itself neutral. What do you do next?"

"Talk with both sides to get the best deal, and then attack for territorial gain!" [buzzer]

"No, Prime Minister, that's quite a poor idea. Italy would be unable to win any decisive battles, would suffer heavy casualties, and would gain little or no territory.

"Let's see if Kaiser Wilhelm of Germany can do better. It's 1917, and the War hasn't been going well, in part due to American supplies being shipped to the Allies. What should you do?"

"Authorize unrestricted submarine warfare against American ships and hope the war can be won before the United States can mobilize?" [buzzer]

"Sorry, Kaiser, but you built too many battleships when you should have been building submarines. Such submarine warfare would not cripple the Allied cause, but it would draw America into the war and lead to a German defeat.

"Next up, we have a team of contestants: President Wilson of the United States, Prime Minister Lloyd George of Britain, and Prime Minister Georges Clemenceau of France. Gentlemen, Germany has been defeated and a treaty to end the war must be drafted. What should the treaty require?"

"It should let Germany have most of its territory, restrict it to having a small army and navy and no air force, and force it to pay reparations to the Allied countries." [buzzer]

"I'm afraid not. That would worsen the economic situation in Germany and increase nationalist feelings in the country while leaving it with an enormous potential for military buildup, which could lead directly to future German aggression.

"Our contestants don't seem to be having much luck today, let's see if British Member of Parliament Winston Churchill can do any better. Mr. Churchill, it is the early 1930s and nationalism is on the rise in India. The Labour government wishes to make concessions, as do many in your own Conservative party. What should you do?"

"Speak out strongly against Indian nationalism and resign from the Conservative shadow Cabinet if my demands aren't met!" [buzzer]

"Very poor choice, Mr. Churchill. Not only is an independent India destined to happen, but such an action on your part would politically isolate you at a time when England might have to remain strong in the face of a dictator in, for example, Germany.

"Now let's hear from Austrian Chancellor Engelbert Dolfuss. Chancellor Dolfuss, the year is 1934 and many Austrians would like to see a union of Austria with Nazi Germany. Italian Premier Benito Mussolini says that he would support Austrian independence only if socialist parties are banned from politics. What should you do?"

"Ban the Communist and Social Democratic parties?" [buzzer]

"No, bad move, Chancellor. I'm afraid that would destroy the one political force with the potential to resist the Nazis. You would probably be murdered by Austrian Nazis, and although Mussolini would protect Austria for a few years, it would inevitably fall to the Nazis and be absorbed by Germany.

"Next we have the Chief of the French Army General Staff, General Maurice Gamelin. General Gamelin, it is 1940 and a German attack on France is inevitable. What are your defense plans?"

"Put most of our forces on the Belgian border, some along the Maginot line, and very few in the wooded Ardennes region, which is of course impassable to a German tank offensive. If the Germans break through our lines they will head towards Paris, and our army will come at them from the rear and catch them in a pincer." [buzzer]

"Well, that all sounds good in principle, but if you do that, the Germans would attack through the lightly defended Ardennes and turn towards the sea, cutting off your forces and throwing your armies into confusion, leading to a complete German victory over France within six weeks.

"It's time to hear from Soviet General Secretary Josef Stalin. The year is 1941 and you have been warned that Germany is about to break the 1939 Nazi-Soviet Non-Aggression Pact. What should you do?"

"Denounce the information as an Allied plot and refuse to make military preparations since this might provoke the Germans!" [buzzer]

"I'm sorry, but Germany is preparing to attack you with more than two million men and your lack of preparation would lead to the capture of most of European Russia as well as millions of Russian troops taken prisoner.

"Now we have with us Prime Minister Fumimaro Konoe of Japan. Prime Minister, your Foreign Minister is urging you to sign a Three-Power Pact with Germany and Italy. What should you do?"

"Sign the pact, which will convince the United States not to involve itself in Asia for fear of becoming involved in a World War." [buzzer]

"No, Prime Minister, signing the pact would only strengthen American resolve and lead to increased U.S. aid to China and an inevitable war with Japan when America would rather be dealing with Germany.

"President Franklin Delano Roosevelt from the United States is next. President Roosevelt, it is November of 1941 and the U.S. Navy has intercepted messages from Tokyo to the Japanese Embassy in Washington indicating that if a diplomatic agreement is not reached between the United States and Japan by November 29, then 'things are automatically going to happen.' Recall that earlier in the year, the U.S. Ambassador to Japan sent a message to the State Department reporting a 'lot of talk around town' that in the event of trouble with the United States, the

Japanese were planning 'a surprise mass attack on Pearl Harbor using all their military facilities.' What should you do?"

"Continue diplomatic negotiations with the Japanese in an attempt to find a compromise acceptable to both sides, and conclude that the probability of a Japanese surprise attack on Pearl Harbor is very small." [buzzer]

"I'm sorry, President Roosevelt, but if you follow that course of action, then on November 25 a Japanese task force would set sail for Hawaii and in the early morning of December 7, the Japanese would send 360 carrier-based planes to destroy two battleships, heavily damage three more, inflict some damage on 14 other ships, damage or destroy 150 planes, and kill more than 3,000 soldiers and sailors at Pearl Harbor.

"Our last contestant is Reich Chancellor Adolf Hitler of Germany. The Japanese have just attacked Pearl Harbor. What should you do?"

"Declare war on America and order a full-scale U-boat attack on American vessels supplying Britain!" [buzzer]

"No, Chancellor, that's not a good idea. Your submarine forces would not be up to the task. Had the resources you put into battleships gone into submarines instead, this might have worked, but as it is, Britain would be able to survive and the economic and military might of the United States would be brought to bear against you, leading to your defeat.

"I'm afraid that none of our contestants have correctly answered any questions, so the grand prize of World Domination will not be awarded this time around. Tune in next time to 'The World at War' to see if one of our new contestants can win the grand prize!"

FISSION EXPLOSIONS

In Which
Humans Develop Nuclear Weapons

(UNCLASSIFIED)

**THIS DOCUMENT CONTAINS   1 PAGE(S).
THIS IS COPY 48032   OF   299792.**

What to do if you want a fission explosion:

1) Get someone to set off an atomic bomb. Convince one or more of the countries that have atomic weapons to detonate one where and when you like. This would probably be difficult to do, unless you happen to want a fission explosion on a small island in the Pacific, in a desert, or near a border between two countries that have recently announced that they have nuclear weapons.

2) Buy an atomic bomb. One or more of the countries that have atomic weapons may be willing to part with a few for the right price.

3) Build an atomic bomb. You could use uranium (in particular, U-235), but this is difficult to obtain since more than 99% of uranium is U-238, which isn't suitable for use as an active material in bombs. Try using plutonium instead. You will need ■■ pounds of either weapons-grade plutonium (90%Pu-239, 10% Pu-240) or reactor-grade plutonium (50% Pu-239, 20% Pu-241, 30% Pu-240). Although the weapons-grade device will reliably release ■■ kilotons of energy, the reactor-grade device will have a less predictable yield of between ■■ and ■■ kilotons. Despite this disadvantage, you will probably have a much easier time obtaining the reactor grade plutonium.

First, assemble a ■■■ cm radius sphere of beryllium surrounded by a ■■ mm-thick layer of gold and ■■■■■■ ■■■■ of polonium. Construct a spherical shell around this sphere with ■■ wedge-shaped grooves on the inside of the shell. The grooves should be covered by a ■■ mm-thick layer of gold and ■■■■■■■■■ of polonium. Then make ■■ identical plutonium wedges and assemble them into a soccer ball shape surrounding the spherical shell. Put conventional explosives around the plutonium shell and a ■■ cm thick shell of uranium-238 around the explosives. Finally, it would be good to have a lead shell around the whole thing to cut down on the radiation coming from the plutonium and uranium before the bomb is detonated.

To activate the bomb, detonate all the conventional explosives simultaneously(within ■■ millionths of a second.) This can be accomplished by ■■■■■■■■■■■■■■

■■■■■■■■■■■■■■■■■■■■■■■■■■■■■■■■■■■■
■■■■■■■■■■■■■■■■■■■■■■■■■■■■■■■■■■■■
■■■■■■■■■■■■■■■■■■■■■■■■■■■■■■■■ The
plutonium wedges will be forced together into a sphere
and the shock will break the beryllium shell along the
grooves, exposing the polonium. Polonium is radioactive
and emits helium nuclei. When beryllium absorbs helium
nuclei, it emits neutrons. When a plutonium atom
absorbs a neutron, it splits into two smaller atoms
(for example, strontium and barium), which releas energy and several more neutrons. These neutrons each go
on to split other plutonium atoms, which emit more
energy and neutrons. Since uranium-238 is a very good
reflector of neutrons, any neutrons that escape from
the plutonium sphere will be bounced back by the uranium shell. The chain reaction continues until between
■% and ■■% of the plutonium atoms have been split, at
which point so much energy has been released that the
bomb (and much of the surrounding countryside) is
vaporized.

4) Just say no. The surgeon general has determined that
fission explosions may be hazardous to your health.

(UNCLASSIFIED)

COMPUTERIZATION

In Which
Computers Become Ubiquitous

```
syslogd 1.3-3: restart.
Console: colour VGA+ 80x25, 1 virtual console (max 63)
pcibios_init : PCI BIOS revision 2.10 entry at 0xfd831
Calibrating delay loop.. ok - 39.73 BogoMIPS
IP Protocols: IGMP, ICMP, UDP, TCP
VFS: Diskquotas version dquot_5.6.0 initialized
Serial driver version 4.13 with no serial options enabled
tty00 at 0x03f8 (irq = 4) is a 16550A
Ramdisk driver initialized : 16 ramdisks of 4096K size
ide: BM-DMA feature is not enabled (BIOS)
hda: WDC AC21000H, 1033MB w/128kB Cache, CHS=525/64/63
hdc: CD-ROM CDR-S1G
ide0 at 0x1f0-0x1f7,0x3f6 on irq 14
scsi : 0 hosts detected total.
Partition check: hda1 hda2 hda3 hda4
VFS: Mounted root (ext2 filesystem) readonly.
Adding Swap: 34268k swap-space (priority -1)
SB 4.13 detected OK (220)
Installed 0

Press a key to continue... Sorry, wrong key.

System going down IMMEDIATELY.

No more processes in runlevel 0.

SYSTEM HALTED.
```

SPACE EXPLORATION

In Which
Humans Begin to Explore Outer Space

_____

"We choose to go to the moon. We choose to go to the
moon in this decade and do the other things, not because
they are easy, but because they are hard, because that goal
will serve to organize and measure the best of our ener-
gies and skills, because that challenge is one that we are
willing to accept, one we are unwilling to postpone, and
one which we intend to win."

> —John F. Kennedy
> 35th President of the United States

"[It's] time for the human race to enter the solar system."

> —J. Danforth Quayle,
> 44th Vice President of the United States

On October 4, 1957, the Soviet Union launched Sputnik I, the first artificial satellite.* The first American satellite—Explorer I—was launched on January 31, 1958, and the Space Race was on! On April 12, 1961, Yury Gagarin became the first human in space, making a one-orbit flight; John Glenn did three orbits on February 20, 1962. Dozens of people and thousands of satellites have followed these pioneers into Earth orbit. The satellites study the Earth, transmit telephone calls between continents, make observations of the Universe, and allow anyone in the world with a satellite dish and a descrambler to watch soap operas and dirty movies.

We've sent spacecraft to study the Moon, the Sun, Mercury, Venus, Earth, Mars, Jupiter, Saturn, Uranus, Neptune, and comets and asteroids. Probes have landed on the Moon, Venus, and Mars, and one has descended into the upper atmosphere of Jupiter (see the table on the following pages).

What will we do next?

Will we complete the space station and start building solar power satellites to capture energy from sunlight and beam it down to Earth, in order to decrease or eliminate the need to burn fossil fuels for electricity?

Will we harvest nearby asteroids? An asteroid six miles on a side would satisfy the current world demand for aluminum, chromium, and gold for twenty to thirty thousand years. At current prices, the gold alone in one such asteroid would be worth about 60 trillion dollars.

Will we invest in a program to detect and divert potentially catastrophic comets and asteroids so that we can avoid the fate of poor Shelley Shrew? Such impacts occur on the Earth every 100 million years or so, and they are quite capable of completely destroying human civilization. It is possible that life on a planet like the Earth will keep mutating and evolving until it develops a species intelligent enough to invest in a program to detect and divert potentially catastrophic comets and asteroids. Remember the wise words of a former vice president of the United States: "If we do not succeed, then we run the risk of failure."

---

*In fact, the first artificial object in space had been launched by accident several months earlier when a manhole cover was left on a 500 foot deep hole during a nuclear test. High speed cameras determined that the velocity of the object right after the blast was more than 40 miles/sec. This velocity is high enough for the manhole cover to have escaped not only from the Earth, but also from the Solar System.

Space missions to other worlds

Date	Mission	Type	Notes
Mar 3, 1959	Pioneer 4	Lunar flyby	first lunar flyby
Sep 15, 1959	Luna 2	Lunar hard landing	first image of lunar farside
Oct 4, 1959	Luna 3	Lunar flyby	
Feb 12, 1961	Venera 1	Venus flyby	first Venus flyby
Jan 26, 1962	Ranger 3	Lunar flyby	
Apr 23, 1962	Ranger 4	Lunar hard landing	
Oct 18, 1962	Ranger 5	Lunar flyby	
Dec 14, 1962	Mariner 2	Venus flyby	
Apr 2, 1963	Luna 4	Lunar orbit	
Jan 30, 1964	Ranger 6	Lunar hard landing	
Apr 2, 1964	Zond 1	Venus flyby	
Jun 28, 1964	Ranger 7	Lunar hard landing	
Feb 17, 1965	Ranger 8	Lunar hard landing	
Mar 21, 1965	Ranger 9	Lunar hard landing	
May 9, 1965	Luna 5	Lunar hard landing	failed soft landing
Jun 8, 1965	Luna 6	Lunar flyby	failed soft landing
Jul 14, 1965	Mariner 4	Mars flyby	first closeup Mars photos
Oct 4, 1965	Luna 7	Lunar hard landing	failed soft landing
Nov 12, 1965	Venera 2	Venus flyby	comm failure
Nov 16, 1965	Venera 3	Venus hard landing	comm failure
Dec 3, 1965	Luna 8	Lunar hard landing	failed soft landing
Dec 16, 1965	Pioneer 6	Solar orbit	
Feb 3, 1966	Luna 9	Lunar soft landing	first soft landing on moon
Mar 31, 1966	Luna 10	Lunar orbit	
Apr 30, 1966	Surveyor 1	Lunar soft landing	
Aug 10, 1966	Lun Orbiter 1	Lunar orbit	
Aug 17, 1966	Pioneer 7	Solar orbit	
Aug 24, 1966	Luna 11	Lunar orbit	
Sep 20, 1966	Surveyor 2	Lunar hard landing	failed soft landing
Oct 22, 1966	Luna 12	Lunar orbit	
Nov 6, 1966	Lunar Orbiter 2	Lunar orbit	
Dec 21, 1966	Luna 13	Lunar soft landing	
Feb 5, 1967	Lunar Orbiter 3	Lunar orbit	
Apr 17, 1967	Surveyor 3	Lunar soft landing	
May 4, 1967	Lunar Orbiter 4	Lunar orbit	
Jul 14, 1967	Surveyor 4	Lunar hard landing	failed soft landing
Jul 19, 1967	Explorer 35	Lunar orbit	

Aug 1, 1967	Lunar Orbiter 5	Lunar orbit	
Sep 8, 1967	Surveyor 5	Lunar soft landing	
Oct 18, 1967	Venera 4	Venus atmospheric probe	
Oct 19, 1967	Mariner 5	Venus flyby	
Nov 7, 1967	Surveyor 6	Lunar soft landing	
Dec 13, 1967	Pioneer 8	Solar orbit	
Jan 7, 1968	Surveyor 7	Lunar soft landing	
Apr 7, 1968	Luna 14	Lunar orbit	
Sep 14, 1968	Zond 5	Lunar flyby	
Nov 8, 1968	Pioneer 9	Solar orbit	
Nov 10, 1968	Zond 6	Lunar flyby	
Dec 21, 1968	Apollo 8	Lunar orbit	3 crew members in orbiter
May 16, 1969	Venera 5	Venus atmospheric probe	
May 17, 1969	Venera 6	Venus atmospheric probe	
May 18, 1969	Apollo 10	Lunar orbit	3 crew members in orbiter
Jul 13, 1969	Luna 15	Lunar hard landing	failed soft landing
Jul 20, 1969	Apollo 11	Lunar soft landing	first person lands on moon
Jul 31, 1969	Mariner 6	Mars flyby	
Nov 19, 1969	Apollo 12	Lunar soft landing	2 crew members in lander
Apr 11, 1970	Apollo 13	Lunar flyby	failed soft landing
Aug 5, 1969	Mariner 7	Mars flyby	
Sep 12, 1970	Luna 16	Lunar soft landing	sample return
Nov 10, 1970	Luna 17	Lunar soft landing	included automated rover
Dec 15, 1970	Venera 7	Venus soft landing	first soft landing on another planet
Feb 5, 1971	Apollo 14	Lunar soft landing	2 crew members in lander
Jul 30, 1971	Apollo 15	Lunar soft landing	2 crew & rover in lander
Sep 2, 1971	Luna 18	Lunar hard landing	failed soft landing
Sep 28, 1971	Luna 19	Lunar orbit	
Nov 13, 1971	Mariner 9	Mars orbit	
Nov 27, 1971	Mars 2	Mars orbit	
Nov 27, 1971	Mars 2	Mars hard landing	failed soft landing
Dec 2, 1971	Mars 3	Mars orbit	
Dec 2, 1971	Mars 3	Mars soft landing	first soft landing on Mars
Feb 14, 1972	Luna 20	Lunar soft landing	sample return
Apr 21, 1972	Apollo 16	Lunar soft landing	2 crew & rover in lander
Jul 22, 1972	Venera 8	Venus soft landing	
Dec 7, 1972	Apollo 17	Lunar soft landing	2 crew & rover in lander

Jan 8, 1973	Luna 21	Lunar soft landing	included automated rover
Jun 10, 1973	Explorer 49	Lunar orbit	
Dec 1, 1973	Pioneer 10	Jupiter flyby	first flyby of Jupiter
Feb 1, 1974	Mars 4	Mars flyby	failed orbit
Feb 2, 1974	Mars 5	Mars orbit	
Feb 5, 1974	Mariner 10	Venus flyby	
Mar 6, 1974	Mars 7	Mars flyby	failed orbit & soft landing
Mar 12, 1974	Mars 6	Mars orbit	
Mar 12, 1974	Mars 6	Mars hard landing	failed soft landing
Mar 29, 1974	Mariner 10	Mercury flyby	first Mercury flyby
May 29, 1974	Luna 22	Lunar orbit	
Sep 21, 1974	Mariner 10	Mercury flyby	
Oct 28, 1974	Luna 23	Lunar hard landing	
Dec 1, 1974	Pioneer 11	Jupiter flyby	
Dec 10, 1974	Helios	Solar orbit	
Mar 16, 1975	Mariner 10	Mercury flyby	
Oct 22, 1975	Venera 9	Venus orbit	
Oct 25, 1975	Venera 10	Venus orbit	
Nov 22, 1975	Venera 9	Venus soft landing	
Nov 25, 1975	Venera 10	Venus soft landing	
Jun 19, 1976	Viking 1	Mars orbit	
Jul 20, 1976	Viking 1	Mars soft landing	
Jul 24, 1976	Viking 2	Mars orbit	
Aug 7, 1976	Viking 2	Mars soft landing	
Aug 9, 1976	Luna 24	Lunar soft landing	sample return
Aug 12, 1978	ICE	Comet Giacobini-Zinner	first comet flyby
Dec 4, 1978	Pioneer 12	Venus orbit	
Dec 9, 1978	Pioneer 13	Venus atmospheric probe	
Dec 21, 1978	Venera 12	Venus soft landing	
Dec 25, 1978	Venera 11	Venus soft landing	
Mar 5, 1979	Voyager 1	Jupiter flyby	
Jul 9, 1979	Voyager 2	Jupiter flyby	
Sep 1, 1979	Pioneer 11	Saturn flyby	first Saturn flyby
Nov 12, 1980	Voyager 1	Saturn flyby	
Aug 26, 1981	Voyager 2	Saturn flyby	
Mar 1, 1982	Venera 13	Venus soft landing	
Mar 5, 1982	Venera 14	Venus soft landing	
Oct 10, 1983	Venera 15	Venus orbit	

Oct 14, 1983	Venera 16	Venus orbit	
Jun 11, 1985	Vega 1	Venus flyby	
Jun 11, 1985	Vega 1	Venus soft landing	
Jun 11, 1985	Vega 1	Venus atmospheric probe	
Jun 15, 1985	Vega 2	Venus flyby	
Jun 15, 1985	Vega 2	Venus soft landing	
Jun 15, 1985	Vega 2	Venus atmospheric probe	
Jan 24, 1986	Voyager 2	Uranus flyby	first Uranus flyby
Mar 1, 1986	Sakigake	Comet Halley flyby	
Mar 6, 1986	Vega 1	Comet Halley flyby	
Mar 8, 1986	Suisei	Comet Halley flyby	
Mar 9, 1986	Vega 2	Comet Halley flyby	
Mar 13, 1986	Giotto	Comet Halley flyby	
Jan 30, 1989	Phobos 2	Mars orbit	
Jan 30, 1989	Phobos 2	Phobos flyby	failed soft landing on a Martian moon
Aug 26, 1989	Voyager 2	Neptune flyby	first Neptune flyby
Feb 10, 1990	Galileo	Venus flyby	
Jan 24, 1990	Muses-A	Lunar orbit	
Aug 10, 1990	Magellan	Venus orbit	
Oct 6, 1990	Ulysses	Solar orbit	
Dec 8, 1990	Galileo	Lunar flyby	
Oct 29, 1991	Galileo	Gaspra flyby	first asteroid flyby
Feb 8, 1992	Ulysses	Jupiter flyby	
Jul 10, 1992	Giotto	Comet Grigg-Skjellerup flyby	
Dec 8, 1992	Galileo	Lunar flyby	
Aug 21, 1993	Mars Observer	Mars flyby	failed Mars orbit
Oct 28, 1993	Galileo	Ida flyby	asteroid flyby
Feb 19, 1994	Clementine	Lunar orbit	
Dec 2, 1995	SOHO	Solar orbit	
Dec 7, 1995	Galileo	Jupiter orbit	first Jupiter orbit
Dec 7, 1995	Galileo	Jupiter atmospheric probe	
Jun 27, 1997	NEAR	Mathilde flyby	asteroid flyby
Jul 4, 1997	Mars Pathfinder	Mars soft landing	included automated rover
Sep 11, 1997	Mars Global Surveyor	Mars orbit	
Jan 11, 1998	Lunar Prospector	Lunar orbit	

POPULATION EXPLOSION

In Which
the Human Population of the Earth
Increases at a Very Rapid Pace

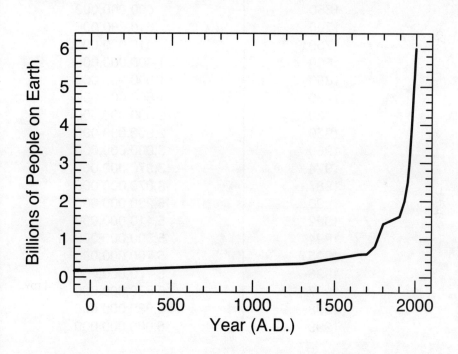

The specifics

DATE	POPULATION
(B.C.) 1,000,000	100,000
300,000	1,000,000
30,000	3,000,000
10,000	4,000,000
4,000	7,000,000
2,000	27,000,000
(A.D.) 1	170,000,000
1000	320,000,000
1300	360,000,000
1650	600,000,000
1700	610,000,000
1750	810,000,000
1800	1,400,000,000
1850	1,500,000,000
1900	1,600,000,000
1930	2,000,000,000
1950	2,500,000,000
1960	3,000,000,000
1974	3,970,000,000
1987	5,070,000,000
1990	5,230,000,000
1992	5,410,000,000
1994	5,600,000,000
1995	5,700,000,000
1996	5,770,000,000
1997	5,850,000,000
1998	5,930,000,000
1999	6,000,000,000

SUPERPOWER CONFRONTATION

In Which
Two Powerful Nations Risk it All

There are, at the present time, two great nations in the world which seem to tend towards the same end, although they started from different points: I allude to the Russians and the Americans . . . . All other nations seem to have nearly reached their natural limits, and only to be charged with the maintenance of their power; but these are still in the act of growth; all others are stopped, or continue to advance with extreme difficulty; these are proceeding with ease and with celerity along a path to which the human eye can assign no term . . . . Their starting point is different, and their courses are not the same; yet each of them seems to be marked out by the will of Heaven to sway the destinies of half the globe. —Alexis de Tocqueville, 1835

"Are you glad to be going off-shift, Commander Procnab?"

"Yes, sub-lieutenant Ratserc, I am, although I'm not sure that our replacements will be as kind to the Earthlings as we have been. Have you finished the report on potential Soviet nuclear weapons mishaps?"
"Yes, sir. Would you like me to review it with you?"

"No, I'll read it later. But I would like a summary of some of the potential American mishaps, in particular, the events related to the Cuban Missile Crisis."

"As you know, that leaves out a lot since the current Earth year is 1999 and we have been on station since 1949, but that crisis is certainly the most extensive that has occurred during our watch. On October 15, 1962, photos of Cuba taken from an American U-2 spyplane revealed nuclear-capable Soviet missiles that would have been able to reach much of the United States. Many of President Kennedy's closest advisors supported an immediate invasion of the island, not knowing that the Soviet field commanders in Cuba had 98 tactical nuclear weapons that could very well have been used against an American invasion force. On October 22, President Kennedy increased military alert to DEFCON 3."

"That involved moving nuclear-equipped interceptors from their home bases to airfields around the country, did it not?"

"Exactly, and because some of these dispersed airfields lacked the proper personnel and equipment, a number of jets had all the safety devices removed from their nuclear weapons. The individual pilots had the ability, though not the authority, to fire their nuclear-tipped missiles. On the evening of October 22, the President addressed the people of the United States, announcing to the world the presence of Soviet missile bases in Cuba and demanding that they be removed. On October 24, Soviet ships on their way to Cuba were stopped by U.S. Naval vessels. DEFCON 2 was announced, which is higher than any other state of readiness that America's nuclear forces have reached before or since."

"I seem to recall that at the time, the first Minuteman ICBMs had only recently been delivered to their base in Montana."

"Yes, Sir. They had been delivered in September, and on October 24 the missile officers began frantically working to get the missiles online as soon as possible. Because of this rush, a number of safety features had to be by-passed. As a result, individual missile officers had the capability—though again not the authority—to launch the missiles under their command."

"What was the next significant event?"

"Early in the morning on October 25, a U.S. Air Force sentry at a base near Duluth, Minnesota, spotted an intruder climbing the fence. He shot at the intruder and sounded the sabotage alarm, which alerted airfields all over the area to watch for possible saboteurs. At Volk Field in Wisconsin, however, the klaxon signalling a nuclear war went off by mistake. The pilots immediately started their nuclear-armed interceptors and were moving down the runway when an officer drove his vehicle in front of them and ordered them to stop. The base commander had phoned Duluth and found out that it was the sabotage alarm that should have sounded, not the nuclear war klaxon. Had the planes taken off and found any U.S. B-47 or B-52 bombers in the air, it is quite possible that they would have mistaken them for Soviet bombers attacking the United States."

"Was the intruder caught?"

"Yes, the intruder turned out to be a bear."

"What happened after that?"

On the following day, October 26, the U.S. Navy searched the Soviet ship *Marcula* and allowed it to continue on to Cuba after finding no missiles aboard. Meanwhile, Vandenberg Air Force Base launched an ICBM. This was a previously scheduled test, but no one had thought to cancel it, despite the fact that the other nine test missiles had been loaded with nuclear weapons during the previous two days. It was known that the Soviets sometimes had agents watching the base; such agents could easily have been aware of the installation of nuclear weapons on the test missiles without realizing that one of the missiles still had its test package intact."

"How much did the Soviets know?"

"That's in the other report. Would you like me to get that information?"

"I'll look at it later. Please continue."

"On October 27, an American U-2 pilot made a navigational error and ended up in Soviet airspace. The pilot radioed for help, and nuclear-armed Air Force F-105 jets were scrambled to escort the pilot back. The Soviets launched interceptors to shoot down the U-2, but it returned to American airspace before they could reach it. Had the U-2 been attacked, it would have been within the local Air Force base commander's authority to order the F-105s to use nuclear missiles against the Soviet aircraft. The interceptor pilots had the ability and, in the case of a communications failure, the authority to attack hostile Soviet aircraft by using their nuclear-tipped missiles. That same day, another U-2 was shot down over Cuba, despite the fact that the Soviet commander on site lacked the authority from Moscow to order such an attack."

"Was that the final incident of the crisis?"

"Not quite. On the morning of October 28, U.S. early warning radar picked up a missile launch from Cuba and predicted an impact in Florida. No impact occurred, however, and it was discovered that a test exercise tape had been accidentally inserted into the operational computer system. Also, a satellite had come over the horizon at just the wrong moment, resulting in a real radar detection despite the fictional missile. Later that day, Soviet Premier Nikita Khruschev announced via Radio Moscow that all nuclear missiles in Cuba would be dismantled."

"Did we play any part in convincing the Soviets to back down?"

"No. Had the Earthlings wanted a nuclear war, they would have gotten one."

"How much of a part did we play in making sure that none of the accidents you described led to an unintended nuclear war?"

"I'll have to go back and check the log. For the record though, we do have the authority—though not the obligation—to prevent accidental nuclear war on the Earth during our watch."

"Of course. I certainly hope that Knabsnoitan is more liberal in interpreting these directives than he used to be. The organisms of Tau Ceti 4 were such a promising species before he let them destroy themselves by accident. I do hope that he doesn't take offense at the shortsighted way that the Earthlings have stored dates in their computer programs until now."

"That's not our problem, Sir."

"True, true, but I do worry about these Earthlings. I've grown rather fond of them during the last fifty years. I'm sure they'll be smart enough to solve their year 2000 problems ahead of time."

"Whatever you say, Sir."

INTERNET EXPANSION

In Which
a Network of Computers Develops

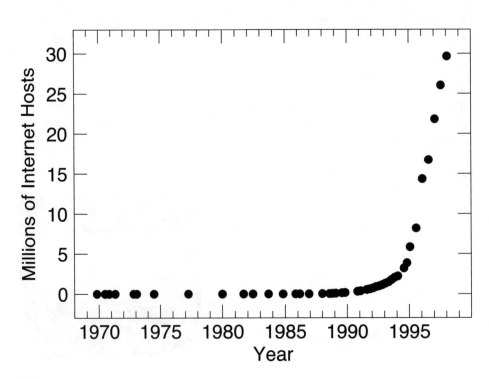

More specifics

Date	Number of Internet Hosts	Date	Number of Internet Hosts
1969	4	1991	376,000
1970	9	1991	535,000
1970	11	1991	617,000
1971	23	1992	727,000
1972	31	1992	890,000
1973	35	1992	992,000
1974	62	1992	1,136,000
1977	111	1993	1,313,000
1980	188	1993	1,486,000
1981	213	1993	1,776,000
1982	235	1993	2,056,000
1983	562	1994	2,217,000
1984	1,024	1994	3,212,000
1985	1,961	1994	3,864,000
1986	2,308	1995	5,846,000
1986	5,089	1995	8,200,000
1988	28,174	1996	14,352,000
1988	33,000	1996	16,729,000
1988	56,000	1997	21,819,000
1989	80,000	1997	26,053,000
1989	130,000	1998	29,670,000
1989	159,000	1998	36,739,000
1990	313,000		

RESIGNATION

In Which
One Human Quits His Job

———————————

[NIXON:]
". . . they [the Brookings Institution] have a lot of material . . . . I want Brookings. I want them just to break in and take it out. Do you understand?"
[HALDEMAN:]
"Yeah. But you have to have somebody to do it."
[NIXON:]
"That's what I'm talking about. Don't discuss it here. You talk to [E. Howard] Hunt. I want the break-in. Hell, they do that. You're to break into the place, rifle the files, and bring them in.
[HALDEMAN:]
"I don't have any problems with breaking in. It's a Defense Department approved security. . ."
[NIXON:]
"—Just go in and take it. Go in around 8:00 or 9:00."

> —Conversation between President Richard Nixon and his
> Chief of Staff, H. R. Haldeman, transcribed by Stanley I.
> Kutler and published in *Abuse of Power*.

A Brief History of Watergate

JUNE 17: Five men are arrested for breaking into a national party head-quarters at the Watergate office-apartment-hotel complex.

JUNE 18: The President's campaign manager—and former Attorney General—holds a press conference, at which he says, "there is no place in our campaign or in the electoral process for this type of activity, and we will not permit or condone it."

JUNE 19: The President's press secretary describes Watergate as "a third-rate burglary attempt" but says that "certain elements may try to stretch this beyond what it is."

JULY 19: In a conversation with his chief domestic affairs advisor, the President says, "If you cover up, you are going to get caught."

August 29: The President holds a press conference at which he notes that "what really hurts in matters of this sort is not the fact that they occur, because overzealous people in campaigns do things that are wrong. What really hurts is if you try to cover it up."

SEPTEMBER 8: In a conversation with an aide, the President says, "The cover-up is what hurts you, not the issue. It's the cover-up that hurts."

OCTOBER 18: The President's press secretary says that no one at "the White House directed activities involving sabotage, spying and espionage."

NOVEMBER 7: The President is re-elected with 60.8% of the vote.

JANUARY 15: Four Watergate defendants plead guilty to the break-in.

JANUARY 28: The President's approval rating is 68%, his highest ever.

FEBRUARY 2: The judge in the Watergate trial says that he is "not satisfied" that the full story was disclosed.

FEBRUARY 7: The Senate votes 70 to 0 to establish a Select Committee to investigate Watergate.

FEBRUARY 22: In a conversation with the vice-chair of the Senate Select Committee on Watergate, the President says, "The main thing is to have no damn cover-up. That's the worst that can happen."

MARCH 14: In a conversation with the White House counsel, the President says, "[E]spionage and sabotage is illegal only if against the government. Hell, you can espionage and sabotage all you want, unless you use illegal means . . . . Can I get away with it?"

MARCH 16: In a conversation with the White House chief of staff, the President says, "The one thing you have to bear in mind is there's only one thing worse than having any substantive disclosures that have not come out, and that is to have the cover-up exposed."

MARCH 19: In a letter to the Watergate judge, one of the defendants writes that he and the other defendants were under "political pressure" to plead guilty and remain silent. He claims that higher-ups were involved in the break-in and that perjury had been committed at the trial.

APRIL 25: In a conversation with the Attorney General, the President says, "I don't want any cover-ups of anything. You know that."

APRIL 27: The acting Director of the FBI resigns after it is revealed that he destroyed evidence relating to the Watergate scandal.

APRIL 30: The White House announces the resignations of the Assistant Secretary of Commerce, the President's chief domestic affairs adviser, the White House chief of staff, the U.S. Attorney General, the White House counsel, and the Undersecretary of Transportation. The President concedes that there "had been an effort to conceal the facts."

MAY 11: In a conversation with the new White House chief of staff and the old White House chief of staff, the President says, "I'm not covering anything up."

OCTOBER 12: The Vice-President resigns and the House minority leader is nominated to replace him.

OCTOBER 20: The new Attorney General and deputy Attorney General resign after refusing to fire the special prosecutor. The Solicitor General is named acting Attorney General and fires the special prosecutor.

NOVEMBER 17: In a televised program from DisneyWorld, the President says that "in all of my years of public life I have never obstructed justice. People have got to know whether or not their President is a crook. Well, I am not a crook. I earned everything I've got."

DECEMBER 6: During hearings about the 18-1/2 minute gap in a crucial taped conversation, the White House chief of staff suggests that "perhaps some sinister force had come in and applied the other energy source and taken care of the information on the tape." Attorneys from the special prosecutor's office suggest that the 18-1/2 minute gap may have been caused by the President.

JANUARY 30: In his State of the Union Address, the President says, "I want you to know that I have no intention whatever of walking away from the job that the American people elected me to do for the people of the United States."

APRIL 30: The President releases 1254 pages of transcripts of taped events within the White House in lieu of turning over the tapes themselves. There are many cases of (expletive deleted), (adjective deleted), and (unintelligible).

JULY 24: The Supreme Court rules 8-0 that the President must turn over 64 tapes sought by the special prosecutor.

JULY 27-30: The House Judiciary Committee passes three articles of impeachment against the President.

AUGUST 9: The President resigns.

THE WHITE HOUSE

WASHINGTON

August 9, 1974

Dear Mr. Secretary:

I hereby resign the Office of President of the
United States.

Sincerely,

Richard Nixon

11.35 AM

HK

The Honorable Henry A. Kissinger
The Secretary of State
Washington, D.C. 20520

REUNIFICATION

In Which
a Country Is Split in Two
and then Becomes One Again

"It is almost never when a state of things is the most detestable that it is smashed, but when, beginning to improve, it permits men to breathe, to reflect, to communicate their thoughts with each other, and to gauge by what they already have the extent of their rights and their grievances. The weight, although less heavy, seems then all the more unbearable."
— Alexis de Tocqueville, September 23, 1853

1945: After the end of World War II, Berlin and Germany are divided into four sectors occupied by the Soviets, Americans, British, and French

"From Stettin in the Baltic to Trieste in the Adriatic, an iron curtain has descended across the continent."
— Winston Churchill, March 5, 1946

1949: Germany is divided into East Germany and West Germany

"Every gun that is fired, every warship launched, every rocket fired, signifies, in the final sense, a theft from those who hunger and are not fed,

those who are cold and are not clothed. The world in arms is not spending money alone. It is spending the sweat of its laborers, the genius of its scientists, the hopes of its children."
—Dwight D. Eisenhower, April, 1953

"Whether you like it or not, history is on our side. We will bury you!"
—Nikita Khrushchev, November 17, 1956

"Let every nation know, whether it wishes us well or ill, that we shall pay any price, bear any burden, meet any hardship, support any friend, oppose any foe to assure the survival and the success of liberty."
—John F. Kennedy, January 20, 1961

1961: The Berlin Wall goes up

"There is no Soviet domination of Eastern Europe. . . . I don't believe that the Rumanians consider themselves dominated by the Soviet Union. I don't believe that the Poles consider themselves dominated by the Soviet Union."
—Gerald Ford, October 6, 1976

"A strong nation, like a strong person, can afford to be gentle, firm, thoughtful, and restrained. It can afford to extend a helping hand to others. It's a weak nation, like a weak person, that must behave with bluster and boasting and rashness and other signs of insecurity."
—Jimmy Carter, October 14, 1976

"God will not forgive us if we fail."
—Leonid Brezhnev, June, 1979

"The superpowers often behave like two heavily armed blind men feeling

their way around a room, each believing himself in mortal peril from the other, whom he assumes to have perfect vision."
—Henry Kissinger, September 30, 1979

"If Washington proves unable to rise above primitive anticommunism, if it persists in a policy of threat and dictate, well, we are sufficiently strong and we can wait. Neither sanctions nor belligerent posturing frighten us."
—Konstantin Chernenko, October 16, 1982

"The present U.S. administration continues to tread an extremely perilous path. . . .It is time they stopped thinking up one option after another in search of the best way of unleashing nuclear war in the hope of winning it. To do this is not just irresponsible, it is madness."
—Yuri Andropov, March 27, 1983

"My fellow Americans: I'm pleased to tell you today that I've signed legislation that will outlaw Russia forever. We begin bombing in five minutes."
—Ronald Reagan, August 11, 1984

"It is better to discuss things, to argue and engage in polemics than make perfidious plans of mutual destruction."
—Mikhail Gorbachev, April 19, 1987

"We are in a war called peace. It is a conflict that has not ended and that will probably continue for generations. The Soviets do not use armies or nuclear weapons to wage this war. Their principal weapons in the struggle with the West are propaganda, diplomacy, negotiations, foreign aid, political maneuver, subversion, covert actions, and proxy war. In this conflict, not only our own freedom but that of the rest of the world are at stake."
—Richard Nixon, January, 1988

"I believe we are on an irreversible trend toward more freedom and democracy—but that could change."
　　　　　　—J. Danforth Quayle, May 22, 1989

"The Cold War began with the division of Europe. It can only end when Europe is whole."
　　　　　　—George Bush, June 1, 1989

"Let's not talk about Communism. Communism was just an idea, just pie in the sky."
　　　　　　—Boris Yeltsin, September 13, 1989

1989: The Berlin Wall comes down

"Today, Eastern Europe is again Central Europe—which it has always been historically, culturally and philosophically."
　　　　　　—Zbigniew Brzezinski, March 7, 1990

1990: Reunification of Germany

"[W]hat I see in Marxist ideology and the Communist pattern of rule is an extreme and cautionary instance of the arrogance of modern man, who styles himself the master of nature and the world, the only one who understands them, the one everything must serve, the one for whom our planet exists. Intoxicated by the achievements of his mind, by modern science and technology, he forgets that his knowledge has limits and that beyond these limits lies a great mystery, something higher and infinitely more sophisticated than his own intellect."
　　　　　　—Václav Havel, October 25, 1991

1991: Dissolution of the Soviet Union

WORLD WIDE WEB CREATION

In Which
a New Medium is Created

"Marc Andreessen will tell you with a straight face that he expects [Netscape] to become the standard interface to electronic information."
              —Gary Wolf, *Wired* (October, 1994)

Come 'n' listen to my story 'bout a kid named Marc,
Poor college student, didn't have a place to park.
An' then one day, after drinking lots of beer,
On his computer he wrote a Web browser.
Mosaic, that is! Pictures! Linked text!

Well, the first thing you know, Marc's a decibillionaire.
Friends all said, "Marc, move away from there."
Said, "Californy is th' place y'oughta be,"
So he packed up a box and he moved to the Valley.
Silicon, that is! Mountain View! Where Sun is!

Young Marc had a company, Lawdy it was hot,
Five million shares sold out in a shot!
Some folks objected: "They don't have any sales!"
But so many used their browser that it was to no avail.
Netscape, that is! Market share! Web dominance!
Well, now it's time to say hello to Bill and Microsoft,

Who never take it lightly if their market share is lost.
Internet Explorer may not be a pretty swap,
But you'll need a lot of help getting it off your desktop.
Lawsuits, that is! DoJ! Questionable business practices!

COMPOSITION

In Which
a Book Is Written

"The greatest part of a writer's time is spent in reading, in order to write; a man will turn over half a library to make one book"
—Samuel Johnson, April 6, 1775

What causes someone to summarize the entire history of the universe in 200 words or less? Boredom and hubris. Let's say you're an astronomer and you're working on a Saturday afternoon because you have more to do than can be fit into a 40-hour workweek. After a few hours of work you realize that you're bored by the details of what you're doing and that you've got to do something different, even if only for an hour or so, or else you'll take "hit any key to continue" far too literally. Even though you know that the end result of your work will be an improved knowledge of the Universe around us, getting to that end result can be a trial at times. While surfing the Internet you find the "History of the United States in 100 Words or Less." The thought crosses your mind that if the history of the United States can be summarized in 100 words, then it should be possible to sum up the history of the universe in 200 words. And who better than you to do it? You are, after all, an astronomer, and cosmology, the study of the origin and history of the universe, is a subfield of astronomy, so you feel quite well qualified to write such a history.

In no time at all, it seems, you've summarized the history of the universe in 200 words or less. Now what do you do with this work? Because you have internalized the philosophy of "publish or perish," you submit the piece to the Internet newsgroup rec.humor.funny, which is read by almost half a million people around the world. Then, 42 minutes later, you receive a missive that begins, "I have accepted your joke for rec.humor.funny." Oh joy, oh rapture, oh bliss. Your work is going to be read by hundreds of thousands of people in dozens of different countries! The piece appears eight weeks later and is brought to the attention of the editor of the *Annals of Improbable Research* (see the glossary entry for more information about this most important scholarly journal), who wants to publish it. Seven months later it appears in that august journal, and nine months after that the editor asks whether you'd like to perform the piece at the Ig Nobel Prize Ceremony, an annual event honoring those whose achievements "cannot or should not be reproduced." The editor has just published *The Best of Annals of Improbable Research*, which contains two of your pieces, and is signing copies of the book at the ceremony. Because of this, two representatives of the publisher are in attendance when you present The History. They ask whether you'd be interested in turning it into a book. After a month or so you've put together a proposal and the publisher has accepted it. Then you find out that you can't write the book after all, because I've already written it. Better luck next time.

Many people have contributed in one way or another to this book. For example, I contributed quite a lot to it. But if it weren't for the people listed below, this book might not exist and certainly wouldn't be what it is. So let's all say "Thank You!" to Marc Abrahams, Emily Anthony, Albert Chou, Caroline Cox, Virginia Cox, William Cox, Garry Diamond, Jim Griffith, David Hyatt, Jonathan Kaplan, Sloane Lederer, John Michel, Regula Noetzli, Emily Schulman, Marvin Schulman, and Ben Zuckerman. Thanks, folks!

EXTRAPOLATION

In Which
Future Events Are Discussed

Extrapolation is a very important concept, but it can be quite difficult to do well. Simply put, extrapolation is trying to figure out what will happen based on what has already happened. Interpolation is easier, that's just using what happened at the start and at the end in order to figure out what happened in the middle. In fact, extrapolation in Irish is *athidirrinneacht*, which literally translated means "getting beyond between points." Let's see what extrapolation can do.

As I write these words it is Feb 13, 1999, and I want to know what the coming year will bring. Since it will take a few months to go from final text to published book, I predict that you are reading these words in the Spring of 1999 or after. You're probably worried about the Year 2000 Problem because the world has less than a year to debug millions of lines of code. That's a pretty scary thought so it would be better not to dwell upon it.

Think instead about your friends and loved ones. A number of them have birthdays coming up—have you thought about what gifts to get them? You know that humorous books make wonderful gifts, but it can be difficult to figure out just what amusing book to give someone who is interested in anthropology, astronomy, biology, chemistry, computer science, earth science, environmental science, history, microbiology, philosophy, physics, political science, psychology, religion, sociology, and/or space science. Relax, the answer is probably right in front of your eyes.

Or perhaps we've reached the year 2000 without the collapse of civilization, and you happen to be one of those noble people who are helping to organize Chicon 2000, the fifty-eighth World Science Fiction Convention, which will be held in Chicago from August 31 until September 4, 2000. You've been thinking about what works to nominate for Hugo Awards. You know what five works you'll nominate for best novel, best novella, best novelette, and of course for best semi-prozine, but gosh darn it, you can't think of an appropriate fifth nominee for best related book. Relax, the answer is probably right in front of your eyes.

Or maybe it's 60 million years A.D. and you've just finished exploring the farthest star in our Milky Way Galaxy. The nearest spiral galaxy to our own is Andromeda, and it's more than 2 million light years away. That's quite a hike, so it would probably be better to radio a message to find out whether anyone's home before going to the trouble of journeying there. The problem is, what should you send to show the Andromedans what wonderful people human beings are? Relax, the answer is probably right in front of your eyes.

GLOSSARY

In Which
Familiar and Unfamiliar Terms Are Defined

Abrahams, Marc: The editor and co-founder of *The Annals of Improbable Research*, the editor of the books *The Best of Annals of Improbable Research* and *Sex As a Heap of Malfunctioning Rubble (and Other Improbabilities)*, and all-around great guy.

Acritarchs: The resting stage of primitive eukaryotic life that lived between 1.8 to 1.5 billion years ago. Acritarchs are always home a-bed.

Aerobic: Reactions that occur in the presence of oxygen. Anaerobic reactions, on the other hand, require the absence of oxygen. Aerobic exercise is good for you, while anaerobic exercise (sprinting, for example) tends to hurt a lot.

Agnosticism: The belief that one is uncertain about whether or not there is a God.

Amino acids: The building blocks of proteins. Although hundreds of amino acids are known, only twenty are used to create proteins in life as we know it. Amino acids have been discovered in meteorites, in the gas between the stars, and in certain hair-care products.

Amish: Followers of the sectarian movement that split from the Anabaptists in 1693, primarily over the Anabaptist belief that only the pure should be involved in religion.

Anabaptists: Members of Christian sects who believe that baptism should only be administered to believers and that infant baptism is not authorized by the Bible.

Ananda Marga Yoga: Founded in 1955, this religion teaches that by meditating several times a day, devotees can reach a state of bliss.

Andropov, Yuri: A river boatman who worked his way up to become General Secretary of the Central Committee of the Communist Party of the Union of Soviet Socialist Republics in 1982.

Anglicans: Members of the Church of England, which split off from Catholicism in 1534 so that Henry VIII could get his marriage to Catherine of Aragon annulled.

Angular momentum: A quality possessed by objects in circular motion, equal to the mass of the body multiplied by its velocity multiplied by the radius of the circle. Angular momentum is "conserved," which means that if the radius decreases, then the velocity increases. A dramatic example of the effects of angular momentum occurs when rotating ice skaters rapidly increase their spin simply by pulling their arms in.

Annals of Improbable Research: A wholly remarkable international science humor magazine, devoted to publishing science articles that are educational and humorous. Call (617-491-4437), write (P.O. Box 380853,Cambridge, MA, 02238, USA), e-mail (air@improbable.com), or open your web browser (http://www.improbable.com) now for subscription information!

Anshar: In Sumerian cosmology he mated with his sister Kishar to create the great gods, including Enki.

Anteater: A mammal that feeds mostly on ants and termites. You probably knew this already, although you may not have thought about the termite part.

Anthony, Emily: Helpful nonscientist critic and good friend from way back in the days of the second Reagan Administration.

Antiparticles: All particles have antiparticles that are identical to them except for having an opposite electromagnetic charge. When particles and antiparticles meet, they annihilate each other and their mass is converted into pure energy as decreed by Einstein's famous formula, $E = mc^2$, where E is energy, m is mass, and c is the speed of light. Many science fiction spaceships run on matter-antimatter engines that use this process.

Arboreal: Living in trees.

Arfvedson, Johann: He discovered lithium in 1817.

Arkwright, Richard: British cotton industry innovator. He built factories to employ hundreds of people, a dramatic change from the situation until then, in which only a few people worked together under one roof.

Arthropods: One of the most successful animal phyla, arthropods makeup more than 75% of all known organisms and include insects, spiders,crustaceans, and trilobites (until they kicked the proverbial bucket).

Assemblies of God: Founded in 1914, it is the largest of the Christian Pentecostal traditions.

Asteroid: Ranging in size from a few miles to more than 500 miles across,asteroids, or "minor planets," are chunks of rock that orbit the Sun and are most common between the orbits of Mars and Jupiter. The author discovered one of these in 1993 but has since lost track of it. Drop me a line if you happen spot minor planet 1993 GZ.

Atheism: The belief that God does not exist.

Atoms: The building blocks of everyday matter, atoms are composed of nuclei surrounded by electrons. The protons and neutrons in the nucleus are held together by the strong nuclear force, and the electrons are bound to the atom by their electromagnetic attraction to the protons in the nucleus. Most hair-care products have large numbers of atoms in them.

Aum Shinrikyo: A belief system that teaches that supreme bliss is attainable through a sequence of initiations after leading a monastic life and severing ties with family and friends. Believers with a knowledge of chemistry are particularly prized.

Aurignacian: A period of time during the Late Stone Age that was characterized by widespread use of flint blades and bone tools. It began around 38,000 B.C. and lasted until about 20,000 B.C.

Austria: A country in central Europe.

Babism: Founded in 1844 by Mirza Ali Muhammad (also called the Bab),this sect of Islam forbid polygamy and was violently persecuted.

Baha'i: Founded in 1863 by Mirza Hoseyn Ali Nuri (a follower of the Bab), the principles of this faith include the oneness of humanity; the oneness of religion; the evolutionary nature of religion; harmony between religion,science, and reason; the elimination of prejudice; the equality of men and women; the abolition of extremes of wealth and poverty; and universal peace.

Baptists: Members of Christian sects who believe that baptism should only be administered to believers and that immersion is the only baptism method authorized by the Bible.

Belgium: A country in western Europe.

Beryllium: Beryllium nuclei have four protons and usually five neutrons.On Earth, a hard gray metal that is sometimes used in golf clubs and nuclear weapons. It emits neutrons when bombarded by helium nuclei.

Berzelius, Jons: He discovered selenium in 1817, silicon in 1823, and thorium in 1828.

Bible: The holy book of Christianity.

Big Bang: The "event" that denotes the origin of our universe.

Billion: A number popularized by the late Carl Sagan, it is written numerically as 1,000,000,000 (or 10^9 in scientific notation). In the United Kingdom, 10^9 is often referred to as "a thousand million," and the word *billion* means 10^{12}, which is what people in the United States call a "trillion."

Bipedal: Having two feet.

Black hole: An object so dense that even light cannot escape from it. Black holes are typically five to a billion times the mass of the sun and spend very little of their time galavanting around the universe gobbling up whatever comes near.

Bosons: Particles with integer spin. Don't worry about it.

Brachiopods: These are marine animals that look like clams, but trust me, there are significant differences that I can't recall at the moment.I'll get back to you on this one.

Branch Davidians: Founded in 1929 as a sectarian movement from the Seventh-Day Adventist Association, which was founded as a sectarian movement from the Seventh-

Day Adventist Church, Branch Davidians believe that the Second Coming of Christ is imminent. Parishioners with prior military experience are particularly prized.

Branhamism: This sect was founded in 1946 and split from the Christian Pentecostal Movement in the 1950s. They believe that the first sin occurred when Eve engaged in sexual activities with the Serpent in the Garden of Eden.

Brezhnev, Leonid Ilyich: A graduate of the Dneprodzerzhinsk Metallurgical Institute, his thesis "The Design of Electrostatic Cleaning of Furnace Gasin the F.E. Dzerzhinsk Factory" received a grade of "excellent." He also led the Soviet Union from 1964 until his death in 1982. His favorite game was dominos.

Broken symmetry: This is a somewhat complicated particle physics concept involving rather complicated mathematics. I wouldn't worry too much about it.

Bruderhof: Formed in 1920 out of the Anabaptist tradition, this sect believes that the current society is a system of injustice based on violence, fear, and isolation, and that a new social order based on unity and joy must take its place.

Brzezinski, Zbigniew: National Security Advisor to the President of the United States from 1977 to 1981. Hi, Dr. Brzezinski!

Buddhism: Founded in India around 530 B.C. by Siddhartha Gautama, this religion teaches that existence is suffering, that suffering is caused by craving and attachment, and that nirvana, or the cessation of suffering, can be reached via the eightfold path of right views, right resolve, right speech, right action, right livelihood, right effort, right mindfulness, and right concentration.

Buoyancy: The upward force felt by objects immersed in a fluid. Balloons float in the air because of buoyancy, while the hair of television personalities is buoyant because they use better hair-care products than you do.

Bush, George Herbert Walker: Born in Massachusetts and raised in Connecticut, he went on to become President of the United States of America in 1988.

Calvinism: Founded in the sixteenth century A.D. by John Calvin, this sect of Protestant Christianity teaches that human beings have no free will and that who will go to Heaven is predetermined. One might think that this would encourage people to do whatever they wanted to, but instead it encouraged them to be thrifty and industrious so as to show everyone else that they were destined for salvation.

Cambrian: The geologic period between 544 and 505 million years ago.

Carbohydrates: Organic compounds like starches and sugars that are composed of carbon, oxygen, and hydrogen. Hair-care products sometimes contain carbohydrates.

Carbon: Carbon nuclei have six protons and usually six neutrons. On Earth, pure carbon is either diamond or graphite, one of which is used in jewelry and the other of which is used in pencils, briquets, and other useful items.

Carbon dioxide: A molecule composed of one atom of carbon and two atoms of oxygen. On Earth, a colorless nonflammable gas required for photosynthesis, released by respiration, and used in carbonated beverages. It is a greenhouse gas.

Carbonic acid: H_2CO_3 is produced when carbon dioxide dissolves in water. It is a component of acid rain.

Carlyle, Thomas: Born in Ecclefechan in 1795, this Scottish writer lived on a farm at Craigenputtock for six years; he hated and feared democracy.

Carnivore: An animal that eats mostly other animals.

Carter, James Earl, Jr.: A nuclear engineer and Sunday school teacher who went on to become President of the United States of America in 1976. He was awarded the Nobel Peace Prize in _____ (please fill in the date once the Nobel Committee gets its act together).

Carthage: Founded in 814 B.C., this ancient city state could have been a contender but instead went 0 for 3 in the Punic Wars with Rome (264 to 146 B.C.) and was utterly destroyed as a result.

Catholicism: A direct descendant of the original Christian Church, which believes that Jesus Christ is the Son of God and that by faith in Christ people may obtain salvation and eternal life.

Cavendish, Henry: He discovered hydrogen in 1766.

Cell: In biology, the smallest unit of living things (if we assume viruses to be non-living). Unicellular organisms have only one cell, while multicellular organisms like you can have trillions of cells. Cells reproduce, convert and store energy, manufacture molecules, and are present in most hair care products.

Cell differentiation: The use of subcellular organelles so that each cell can have different duties in multicellular organisms.

Celts: A large group of pre-Roman Europeans.

Ceremonialism: Any of a number of different belief systems that revolve around ordered actions of a symbolic nature performed to express and transmit values and beliefs. You know, ceremonies. The earliest evidence of ceremonial burial dates from about 26,000 B.C.

Cheetah: A very fast carnivorous land mammal.

Chen Tao: Formed in 1993, the followers of Chen Tao believe that the Earth has endured four nuclear holocausts, more than 888,800 million lesser holocausts, and is about to experience a fifth nuclear holocaust.

Chernenko, Konstantin Ustinovich: The head of the agitation and propaganda department of the Moldavian republic between 1948 and 1956, he became the General Secretary of the Central Committee of the Communist Party of the Union of Soviet Socialist Republics in 1984.

Chitin: A white or colorless substance that forms the hard, outer part of crustaceans and insects. Try not to think about it too much.

Chloroplast: An organelle in plants that turns light, carbon dioxide,and water into carbohydrates and oxygen. Health food often includes chloroplasts.

Chordates: The animal phylum that includes humans and other vertebrates,chordates have a dorsal nerve cord that runs down the back and connects the brain with the rest of the body.

Chou, Albert: Plasma-physics-graduate-student-cum-copy-editor, turned software engineer and director of marketing at Maverick Technologies;hopefully one day proprietor of The Random Cafe. "He was a fiddler, and consequently a rogue." —Jonathan Swift

Christadelphianism: Founded in 1844, Christadelphians believe that baptism by immersion after receiving knowledge of the Bible is crucial to salvation.

Christian Reconstructionism: Founded in 1973, this Christian sect believes that all human behavior is inherently religious.

Christian Science: Founded in 1879 by Mary Baker Eddy, Christian Scientists deny the reality of the material world and believe that healing results from understanding one's indestructible relationship with God.

Chromosomes: Thread-like collections of genetic material in cell nuclei.Humans have 23 pairs of chromosomes.

Churchill, Sir Winston Leonard Spencer: Prime Minister of England between 1940 and 1945, he should not be confused with Winston Churchill the American novelist and member of the New Hampshire legislature between 1903 and 1905.

Cigar: A roll of tobacco leaves usually used for smoking.

Clemenceau, Georges: Premier of France in 1906-1909 and 1917-1919, he was also a doctor, a teacher, a journalist, and a novelist.

Cluster of galaxies: A collection of hundreds or thousands of galaxies held together by the gravitational attraction between them.

Cluster of stars: A collection of from hundreds to millions of stars. Globular clusters are stable collections of hundreds of thousands to millions of stars and are held together by gravitational attraction. Open star clusters are smaller and tend to be locations where stars have recently formed; they do not in general survive for more than a few tens of millions of years.

Colonial organism: A colony of unicellular organisms.

Combustion: Burning, whether logs on the fire or hydrocarbons in your automobile.

142

Comet: Dirty snowballs composed mostly of dust plus frozen water, carbon dioxide, ammonia, and methane. They tend to be several miles across and they orbit around the Sun at very large distances,mostly past the orbit of Neptune (more than 30 times farther from the Sun than the Earth is). Every so often one will come into the inner solar system and release a dramatic tail of evaporated ices.

Compiler: A computer program that translates computer programs written in a particular computer language that only programmers can understand into lists of instructions that only computers can understand.

Computer: A device that tends to do what you tell it to rather than what you want it to.

Computer language: The syntax and commands used to give instructions to computers. The statements in computer languages are usually composed of a series of incomprehensible words and symbols that require a compiler to translate them into a series of incomprehensible strings of 1's and 0's.

Condensation: The process by which gas molecules turn into liquid molecules.

Confucianism: The moral and religious system of many people in China, it was founded by K'ung Fu-tse (Confucius) late in the sixth century B.C. It states that everyone must strive to be virtuous and looks forward to the great commonwealth when humanity is united under ethical rule.

Copulation: To engage in . . . hey, how did this word get on the list?

Cox, Caroline: Astronomy Ph.D., excellent copy editor, and all-around wonderful person. Dr. Cox has co-written a number of *Annals of Improbable Research* articles, including "How to Write a Ph.D. Thesis," "How to Write a Scientific Research Report," and "Pat the Dean."

Cox, Virginia: Mother of all-around wonderful person Caroline Cox.

Cox, William: Father of all-around wonderful person Caroline Cox and expert on military history.

Crustaceans: A large class of arthropods that includes crabs, lobsters, shrimp, barnacles, and wood lice. You don't really want to know all about their chitinous exo-skeletons, do you?

Cuba: An island nation in the Western Hemisphere of the planet Earth, famous for its cigars.

Curie, Marie Sklodovska: With Pierre Curie, she discovered polonium and radium in 1898. They were awarded the Nobel Prize for Physics in 1903 and she was awarded the Nobel Prize for Chemistry in 1911.

Cyanobacteria: Blue-green algae. These single-celled organisms use light to produce carbohydrates and oxygen through photosynthesis. The results of their work can be found in most health food stores.

Danes: Natives of Denmark—in this case those who plundered the coasts of Europe in the eighth through tenth centuries A.D.

Deism: The belief that the wonders of nature demonstrate the existence of God and that formal religion is unnecessary and can be counterproductive, given the conflicts between adherents of different religious belief systems.

Denmark: A country in northern Europe.

Deoxyribonucleic acid (DNA): The nucleic acid that contains the genetic code for organisms on the Earth. The fundamental building blocks of DNA are a phosphate (PO_4), a sugar (deoxyribose), and a nucleic acid base (either adenine, thymine, guanine, or cytosine). Some hair care products have DNA in them. According to the Cable News Network, many people first heard about DNA during the Orenthal James Simpson trial.

Deuterium: Heavy hydrogen, with one proton and one neutron in the nucleus. Tritium is even heavier, with two neutrons and one proton in the nucleus. Tritium is somewhat radioactive, so its presence in the congressional districts of influential representatives can lead to highly political government actions, even when the amount of radioactivity is very small.

Deuteron: An atom of deuterium.

Diamond, Garry: Teacher, therapist, and wonderful mother.

Dimitrijevic, Colonel Dragutin: The Chief of the Intelligence Department in the Serbian General Staff who organized the assassination of Archduke Ferdinand in 1914. He had also been involved in the assassination of King Alexander in 1903.

Dinoflagellates: Unicellular organisms that have two long groups of protein strands called "flagella" that are used for locomotion.

Dinosaur: I think you know this one.

Diplomonads: Heterotrophic protists that lack mitochondria.

Discordianism: Founded in 1958, this belief system teaches that the world is a chaotic, confusing, and disordered place that human beings attempt to veil with a thin sheet of order and stability.

Dissociation: The separation of molecules into their component atoms.

Dollfuss, Engelbert: Leader of the Austrian Farmers' League, he became Chancellor of Austria in 1932 and met his untimely end on July 25, 1934,at the hands of Austrian Nazis.

Donnybrook: A suburb of Dublin, Ireland. The Donnybrook Fair was held each year between 1204 and 1855, when it was suppressed because of disruptive brawls and excessive rioting.

Dorn, Fredrich Ernst: He discovered radon in 1898.

Dorn, Michael: He played Lieutenant Worf in 1988.

Druidism: A collection of beliefs from numerous ancient European religions stressing the cultivation of a close relationship with nature and the pursuit of knowledge and wisdom.

Dust: In astronomy, dust refers to very small (about 10 millionths of an inch in diameter) grains of carbon, silicon, and other elements.

Earth: The third planet from the Sun, it has a mass of seven thousand billion billion tons and a diameter of about 8000 miles. It has an atmosphere of nitrogen and oxygen and one relatively large moon. It is very likely to be the planet on which you are reading this book.

Echinoderms: An animal phylum that includes starfish and sea urchins, echinoderms can only live in saltwater.

Eckankar: Founded in 1965, this religion teaches that the body is separate from the immortal inner soul, that people must travel through twelve planes of existence before they can reach God, and that it is important to limit one's use of alcohol, tobacco, and drugs.

Eisenhower, Dwight David: An American general famous for his leadership in World War II who, in 1948, became President of Columbia University.

Electromagnetic force: One of the four fundamental forces of nature, this force results in opposite charges attracting each other (for example, a proton and an electron) and for similar charges repelling each other (for example, two protons). The electromagnetic force is not as strong as the strong nuclear force, which means that atomic nuclei are held together despite the fact that protons repel each other electromagnetically.

Electrons: These particles are negatively charged. They are much less massive than the protons and neutrons that make up the nucleus of atoms. Collecting too many can be a shocking experience.

Endosymbiont: An organism in a symbiotic relationship with the organism within which it is living.

Energy barrier: A region that requires a certain amount of energy to enter. For example, two protons both have positive electric charge and therefore repel each other, with the strength of the repelling force being proportional to the inverse of the square of the distance. In other words, the closer the protons get, the larger the force pushing them apart becomes and the more energy is required to overcome the repelling force. When the two protons are sufficiently close, then the strong nuclear force can hold them together because it is much stronger than the electromagnetic force pushing them apart.

England: A country in western Europe.

Enki: In Sumerian cosmology he was married the goddess Ninki; Marduk was their son.

Episcopalians: Members of American churches that split from the English Anglican Church in 1789.

Evaporation: The process by which liquid molecules turn into gas molecules.

Eukaryotic life: Life made up of cells with nuclei that contain DNA. Such cells often have organelles like mitochondria or chloroplasts. All known plants and animals are eukaryotes, as are fungi and many relatively simple organisms known as protists. Prokaryotic life, on the other hand, lacks discrete nuclei and subcellular organelles. It is likely that you are a eukaryotic organism.

Europe: A continent in the northern hemisphere of the planet Earth.

Exoskeleton: A skeleton that supports the body from the outside rather than from the inside. Try not to think about it too much.

Exponential expansion: A rate of increase that is proportional to the current value. For example, if the universe doubles in size every 10^{-35} seconds, then after the first 10^{-35} seconds it will be twice it's original size, after the second it will be four times, after the third it will be eight times, and after the thousandth (e.g., after 10^{-32} seconds) it will be 10^{300} times its original size. At the moment, the universe is no longer expanding exponentially, but rather in a linear fashion.

Fermions: Particles with half-integer spin. Don't worry about it. Really.

Flagella: Long groups of protein strands used by for locomotion by some microscopic organisms.

Ford, Gerald Rudolph: College football player at the University of Michigan, Park Ranger at Yellowstone National Park, and President of the United States from 1974 until 1977, he was born Leslie Lynch King, Jr. His favorite desert is butter pecan ice cream.

Ford, Henry: A machinist's apprentice who went on to found the Detroit Automobile Company in 1899. That didn't work out too well, so in 1903 he founded the Ford Motor Company, which did rather better.

Four-dimensional: Ah, this is a tricky one. Let's start small. A point has no size at all, it is zero-dimensional. A line is one-dimensional:it has only length. A square is two-dimensional, it has length and width, which are perpendicular to each other. A cube is three-dimensional, it has length, width, and height, which are all perpendicular to each other. A hyper cube is four-dimensional, it has length, width, height, and another dimension perpendicular to the first three. I can't point to this dimension, just as a two-dimensional creature couldn't point out what direction "height" could be measured in.

France: A country in western Europe.

Freemasonry: Formed in 1717, Freemasonry stresses tolerance, respect,kindness, understanding, philanthropy, and morals. Some claim that the Masons are a secret society, although their membership, constitution, rules, aims, and principles are not secret and they sometimes advertise in in-flight magazines.

Fundamentalism: Christian Fundamentalists believe that the Bible is literally true and that they are the guardians of the truth. There are also fundamentalists in other religious traditions.

146

Fusion: The building of heavier elements from lighter ones, a process that usually releases energy. For example, four protons (hydrogen nuclei) combine to form one helium nucleus in hydrogen fusion. The four protons together have more mass than the helium nucleus, and the mass difference is released as energy via Einstein's $E = mc^2$.

Galaxy: A collection of hundreds of billions of stars held together by gravitational attraction. We live in a galaxy called the Milky Way.

Gamov, George: Ukranian-born theoretical physicist and cosmologist whose books include *Mr. Tompkins in Wonderland* and *Mr. Tompkins Explores the Atom*.

Gamelin, Maurice Gustave: Appointed Chief of the French General Staff in 1931, he was named Commander in Chief of all French forces in June of 1939and generalissimo of the Allied forces at the start of World War II in September, 1939. The war didn't go too well for France, though, and he was replaced on May 19, 1940. He spent the war in prison in Germany.

Gas: A state of matter in which the volume expands in all directions unless confined. For example, interstellar matter is a gas.

Geologic time: Geologic time is broken up into eons that lasted between500 and 1500 million years, eras that lasted between 65 and 250 million years, periods that lasted between 2 and 100 million years, and epochs that lasted between 10,000 years and 20 million years. We are currently in the Holocene Epoch (9,000 B.C. onwards) of the Quaternary Period (1.8 million B.C.. onwards) of the Cenozoic Era (65 million B.C. onwards) of the Phanerozoic Eon (544 million B.C. onwards).

Georgia: A country in western Asia. Also, a state in the southeastern United States.

Germany: A country in central Europe.

Gills: Respiratory organs that can extract oxygen from water.

Glossary: A list of words and their definitions, usually found at the back of a book, in which the author tries to explain all potentially unfamiliar terms.Of course, the potentially unfamiliar terms in the glossary definitions then require glossary entries, and the potentially unfamiliar terms in these definitions then require glossary entries. See the entry on recursion.

Gold: Gold nuclei have 79 protons and usually 118 neutrons. On Earth, gold is a metallic element used in jewelry, coins, electronics, and nuclear weapons.

Gorbachev, Mikhail Sergeevich: An assistant combine operator who worked his way up to become General Secretary of the Central Committee of the Communist Party of the Union of Soviet Socialist Republics. He won the Nobel Peace Prize in 1990.

Gravitational force: One of the four fundamental forces of nature, this force results in every particle attracting every other particle. The gravitational attraction between all our particles and all the particles in the Earth keep us on the ground.

Greece: A country in southeastern Europe.

Greenhouse gas: A gas that acts to heat the atmosphere of the Earth ina way that's not as similar as you'd expect to the way that a glass greenhouse heats the air inside of it.

Griffith, Jim: Moderator of the news group rec.humor.funny.

Gurdjieff: Founded in 1913, followers of Gurdjieff believe that all individuals need purification and that they must work on relationships by opening themselves to others.

Habitable zone: The region around a star in which a potentially habitable planet (one with oceans of liquid water) can exist. The more massive the star, the larger the habitable zone is. In our Solar System the habitable zone is between about 88 million miles from the Sun and about 130 million miles from the Sun; the Earth is 93 million miles from the Sun.

Hair care products: Products usually used for caring for one's hair.

Half-integer spin: Please don't ask.

Half-life: The time it takes for half of a quantity of radioactive material to decay. The half-life of radon-222 is 3.8 days, while the half-life of uranium-238 is 4.5 billion years.

Hargreaves, James: Some folks reckon that he invented them spinning jenny things 'round about 1765.

Hasidism: Founded in the early 1700s by Rabbi Israel ben Eliezar, Ba'alShem Tov as a sect of Judaism, Hasidism stresses the priority of emotion over intellect, the idea that all men are equal before God, and that prayerful devotion is preferable to Talmudic Study. It is closely related to Orthodox Judaism.

Hannibal: The greatest general to ever oppose the Roman Empire, Hannibal and his small army invaded Italy in 218 B.C. and ravaged it for 15 years until he was recalled to defend Carthage in 203 B.C.

Havel, Václav: A playwright, essayist, and brewery worker, he became President of the Czech and Slovak Federal Republic in 1989, and the first President of the Czech Republic in 1992.

Helium: The next heaviest element after hydrogen. Helium nuclei have two protons and usually two neutrons. Neutral helium atoms have two electrons. On Earth, helium is a colorless, odorless,non-flammable gas that allows balloons to fly but doesn't result in fiery explosions.

Herbivore: An animal that eats mostly plants.

Heterotroph: An organism that obtains food from outside sources rather than by making it through photosynthesis or other methods. You are probably a heterotroph.

Higgs particles: These as yet undiscovered scalar bosons are purported to give leptons, quarks, and intermediate vector bosons their masses, would be responsible for the existence of nine rather than three charged quark currents, and would cause both parity and charge-parity symmetry violations in weak processes. Are you sorry you asked?

Hinduism: The religious beliefs and practices of the majority of people in India. Its beliefs include reincarnation based on karma, wherein the good and bad actions of individuals determine the form they will take in the next lifetime.

Hitler, Adolf: Would the world have been any different had he been named Adolf Schicklgruber?

Holland: A country in western Europe. See the entry on the Netherlands.

Hopper, Grace Murray: A leader in the field of software development and validation, she developed the first compiler and created the computer language that led directly to COBOL, the first business-oriented programming language. She was born in 1906, studied mathematics and physics at Vassar College, and received a Ph.D. in mathematics from Yale in 1934, while she was a professor at Vassar. In 1943 she joined the United States Naval Reserve as a Lieutenant (Junior Grade) and was the first programmer of the Navy's Mark I computer. While working on the Mark II computer at Harvard she found the first example of an actual bug in a computer. She retired from the Naval Reserve as a Rear Admiral when she was eighty years old and she died in 1992 at the age of eighty-five.

Humanism: Belief systems that emphasize human capabilities, the study of past human achievements and literature, and respect for scientific knowledge.

Huns: A nomadic tribe from Mongolia that took control over a large portion of Europe in the fifth century A.D.

Hyatt, David: Author of *The History of the United States in 100 Words or Less.*

Hydrogen: The most basic chemical element, hydrogen has atoms made up of one proton and one electron. On Earth, hydrogen is a colorless, odorless,flammable gas that allows balloons to fly, burn, and/or explode, depending on the size of the balloon and whether or not there are any sparks nearby.

Hydrogen sulfide: A molecule composed of one atom of sulfur and two atoms of hydrogen. On Earth, hydrogen sulfide is a colorless gas with quite an odor (think rotten eggs).

ICBM: An intercontinental ballistic missile, which is a missile that can launch a warhead from one continent and have it land in another. In practice,ICBMs have ranges of four thousand miles or more.

Ig Nobel Prize: These prizes honor people whose achievements cannot or should not be reproduced. They are given out every October by Marc Abrahams.

Impeachment: The formal presentation of charges against a public official accused of misconduct so that he or she will be tried and removed from office if convicted. For example, Robert Aderholt, Bill Archer, Richard Armey, Spencer Bachus III, Richard Baker,

Cass Ballenger, Bob Barr, Bill Barrett, Roscoe Bartlett, Joe Barton, Charles Bass, Herbert Bateman, Doug Bereuter, Brian Bilbray, Michael Bilirakis, Tom Bliley, Roy Blunt, Sherwood Boehlert, John Boehner, Henry Bonilla, Mary Bono, Kevin Brady, Ed Bryant, Jim Bunning, Richard Burr, Dan Burton, Stephen Buyer, Sonny Callahan, Ken Calvert, Dave Camp, Tom Campbell, Charles Canady, Christopher Cannon, Michael Castle, Steve Chabot, Saxby Chambliss, Helen Chenoweth, Jon Christensen, Howard Coble, Tom Coburn, Michael Collins, Larry Combest, Merrill Cook, John Cooksey, Christopher Cox, Philip Crane, Michael Crapo, Barbarra Cubin,Randy Cunningham, Thomas Davis III, Nathan Deal, Tom DeLay, Lincoln Diaz-Balart, Jay Dickey, John Doolittle, David Dreier, John Duncan, Jr., Jennifer Dunn, Vernon Ehlers, Robert Ehrlich, Jr., Jo Ann Emerson, Phil English, John Ensign, Terry Everett, Thomas Ewing, Harris Fawell, Mark Foley, Michael Forbes,Vito Fossella, Jr., Tillie Fowler, Jon Fox, Bob Franks, Rodney Frelinghuysen, Elton Gallegly, Greg Ganske, George Gekas, Jim Gibbons, Wayne Gilchrest, Paul Gillmor, Benjamin Gilman, Newt Gingrich, Virgil Goode, Jr., Robert Goodlatte, William Goodling, Porter Goss, Lindsey Graham, Kay Granger, James Greenwood,Gil Gutknecht, Ralph Hall, James Hansen, Dennis Hastert, Doc Hastings,J. D. Hayworth, Jr., Joel Hefley, Wally Herger, Rick Hill, Van Hilleary, David Hobson, Peter Hoekstra, Stephen Horn, John Hostettler, Kenny Hulshof, Duncan Hunter, Asa Hutchinson, Henry Hyde, Bob Inglis, Ernest Istook, Jr., William Jenkins,Nancy Johnson, Sam Johnson, Walter Jones, John Kasich, Sue Kelly, Jay Kim, Jack Kingston, Scott Klug, Joe Knollenberg, Jim Kolbe, Ray LaHood, Steve Largent, Tom Latham, Steven LaTourette, Rick Lazio, James Leach, Jerry Lewis, Ron Lewis, John Linder, Bob Livingston, Frank LoBiondo, Frank Lucas, Donald Manzullo, Bill McCollum, Jim McCrery, Joseph McDade, Paul McHale, John McHugh, Scott McInnis, David McIntosh, Howard McKeon, Jack Metcalf, John Mica, Dan Miller,Jerry Moran, Sue Myrick, George Nethercutt, Jr., Mark Neumann, Robert Ney, Anne Meagher Northup, Charlie Norwood, Jim Nussle, Michael Oxley, Ron Packard, Mike Pappas, Mike Parker, Ron Paul, Bill Paxon, Edward Pease, John Peterson, Thomas Petri, Charles Pickering, Jr., Joseph Pitts, Richard Pombo, John Porter,Rob Portman, Deborah Pryce, Jack Quinn, George Radanovich, Jim Ramstad, Bill Redmond, Ralph Regula, Frank Riggs, Bob Riley, James Rogan, Harold Rogers, Dana Rohrabacher, Ileana Ros-Lehtinen, Marge Roukema, Edward Royce, Jim Ryun, Matt Salmon, Marshall Sanford, Jim Saxton, Joe Scarborough, Dan Schaefer, Bob Schaffer, James Sensenbrenner, Jr., Pete Sessions, John Shadegg, E. Clay Shaw, Jr., John Shimkus, Bud Shuster, Joe Skeen, Christopher Smith, Lamar Smith, Linda Smith, Nick Smith, Robert Smith, Vince Snowbarger, Gerald Solomon, Mark Souder, Floyd Spence, Clifford Stearns, Charles Stenholm, Bob Stump, John Sununu, James Talent, W. J. Tauzin, Charles Taylor,

Gene Taylor, William Thomas, William Thornberry, John Thune, Todd Tiahrt, Fred Upton, James Walsh, Zach Wamp, Wes Watkins, J. C. Watts, Jr., Curt Weldon, Dave Weldon,Gerald Weller, Rick White, Edward Whitfield, Roger Wicker, Heather Wilson, Frank Wolf, C. W. Bill Young, and Don Young voted to impeach the President of the United States, William Jefferson Clinton, on December 19, 1998. In the United States, the House of Representatives votes for the impeachment of federal officials while the Senate is responsible for trying them. For example, Spencer Abraham, Wayne Allard, John Ashcroft, Robert Bennett, Christopher Bond, Sam Brownback, Jim Bunning, Conrad Burns, Ben Nighthorse Campbell, Thad Cochran, Paul Coverdell, Larry Craig, Mike Crapo, Mike Dewine, Pete Domenici, Mike Enzi, Peter Fitzgerald, William Frist, Slade Gorton, Phil Gramm, Rod Grams, Chuck Grassley, Judd Gregg, Charles Hagel, Orrin Hatch, Jesse Helms, Tim Hutchinson, Kay Bailey Hutchison, James Inhofe, Jon Kyl, Trent Lott, Richard Lugar, Connie Mack, John McCain, Mitch McConnell, Frank Murkowski, Don Nickles, Pat Roberts, William Roth, Jr., Rick Santorum, Jeff Sessions, Richard Shelby, Bob Smith, Gordon Smith, Ted Stevens, Craig Thomas, Fred Thompson, Strom Thurmond, George Voinovich, and John Warner voted to convict the President of the United States, William Jefferson Clinton, of obstruction of justice on February 12, 1999.

Inflation: In economics, too many dollars chasing too few goods, leading to price increases. In astrophysics, an exponential expansion of the universe that occurred between about 10^{-37} and 10^{-32} seconds after the Big Bang.

Integer-spin: Are you sure you want to know?

Integral Yoga: Founded in 1904, Integral Yoga teaches that people can obtain self-knowledge through regulated breathing, meditation, and/or self surrender.

Ionization: The process of stripping electrons from atoms. Ionized atoms have lost one or more of their electrons, making them positively charged and therefore subject to electric and magnetic fields. If you want tobe picky about it, adding extra electrons to neutral atoms is also considered ionization.

Ireland: A country in western Europe.

Islam: Founded in 622 A.D. by Muhammad, Islam is the principal religion of much of the Middle East and Asia. It teaches that one should submit to the will of God and constantly praise and glorify him.

Italy: A country in southern Europe.

Jainism: Founded by Mahavir Jain in the sixth Century B.C., Jainism is an offshoot of Hinduism and teaches that the cycle of reincarnation and rebirth can be escaped through monastic retreat, charity, and good works toward all life, especially humans and animals. Jainism teaches that the Universe had no beginning, that it will have no end, and that it operates in accordance with natural law.

Jehovah's Witnesses: Founded by Charles Taze Russel in 1869 as a sect of the Adventists, their beliefs include that God's name is Jehovah,that salvation is acquired by good works, that only 144,000 people will enter Heaven, that those who do not make it into Heaven will disappear as if they had never existed, that Satan and his evil angels were kicked out of heaven to rule the Earth in 1914, and that Jesus will return soon. In 1997, 5,599,931 Jehovah's Witnesses in 232 countries spent a total of 1,179,735,841 hours preaching. On average, each Jehovah's Witness spent 34.60693 minutes preaching each day.

Johnson, Samuel: An English writer who published a 40,000-entry *Dictionary of the English Language* in 1755, he should not be confused with the American clergyman who was the first president of King's College (which later became Columbia University).

Johnson, Samuel: An American clergyman who was the first president of King's College (which later became Columbia University), he should not be confused with the English writer who published a 40,000-entry *Dictionary of the English Language* in 1755.

Judaism: The religious beliefs and practices of the Jews. You want to know more? What am I, a rabbi? Jews are seldom more than one of the following: Extremely Orthodox, Orthodox, Very Conservative, Conservative, Somewhat Conservative, Reform, or Extremely Reform.

Jupiter: The fifth planet from the Sun and the largest of the planets in the Solar System. Jupiter is 320 times the mass of the Earth and is 90,000 miles in diameter. It has about twenty moons larger than 10 miles in diameter and four moons larger than 2000 miles in diameter.The Jovian atmosphere is very thick and is composed almost entirely of hydrogen and helium.

Jutes: A Germanic tribe from Jutland, some of whom settled in England in the fifth century A.D.

Kangaroo: A herbivorous marsupial with powerful legs and a long tail.

Kaplan, Jonathan: Professor of Philosophy at the University of Tennessee at Knoxville and good friend from way back in the days of the first Reagan Administration. Professor Kaplan deserves thanks for critically reading a final version of the manuscript and pointing out a number of inconsistencies.Any remaining errors are, of course, entirely his fault.

Kennedy, John Fitzgerald: A Pulitzer Prize-Winning biographer, he was President of the United States from 1961 until his death in 1963. There are many theories about his death, one of the most concise being that a tiger killed him. He should not be confused with J. Danforth Quayle, the Vice President of the United States between 1989 and 1993.

Khrushchev, Nikita: Russian shepherd and locksmith, he was also Premier of the Soviet Union between 1958 and 1964.

Kibology: When asked "How does kibology compare?" James "Kibo" Perry answered "Kibology is better." It is said that while some followers of kibology wear pants, others do not.

Kingdom: In the Linnaean classification scheme used in biology, humans are of the animal kingdom, the chordata phylum, the vertebrata subphylum, the mammalia class, the eutheria subclass, the primate order, the anthropoidea suborder, the hominidae family, the *Homo* genus, and the *sapiens* species.

Kishar: In Sumerian cosmology she mated with her brother Anshar to create the great gods, including Enki.

Kissinger, Henry Alfred: Secretary of State of the United States of America between 1973 and 1977, he was awarded the Nobel Peace Prize in 1973.

Klaproth, Martin: He discovered uranium and zirconium in 1789.

Konoye, Fumimaro: Premier of Japan twice (1937-1939 and 1940-1941), his aim of a "new order in East Asia" didn't come about quite like he imagined.

Lakhamu: In Sumerian cosmology, a primeval serpent who, with Lakhmu, brought forth Anshar and Kishar.

Lakhmu: In Sumerian cosmology, a primeval serpent who, with Lakhamu, brought forth Anshar and Kishar.

Lead: Lead nuclei have 82 protons and usually 125 neutrons. On Earth, lead is a soft gray metal that should not be consumed by humans. Lead consumption can lead to frequent headaches, difficulty concentrating, lethargy, and a host of other maladies. If a friend asks you to eat lead, just say no!

Lederer, Sloane: Trade sales and marketing director at W. H. Freeman and Company Publishers and enjoyable person to work with.

Lieutenant: A relatively low-ranking officer. See the entry on military commissioned officer ranks.

Light-year: The distance that light travels in a year, about 6 trillion miles.

Limestone: Stone that consists mainly of calcium carbonate, $CaCO_3$.

Linear growth: If you deposit \$100 a month in a savings account that pays no interest, and you never withdraw any money, then your savings account is growing linearly. After the first month you have \$100, after the second \$200, after the third \$300, and so on.

Liquid: A state of matter in which the volume is constant, although the shape can change. Hair-care products are sometimes liquid.

Lithium: The next heaviest element after hydrogen and helium. Lithium nuclei have three protons and usually four neutrons. On Earth, lithium is a soft silver metal used in batteries, ceramics, and lubricants. Lithium carbonate can help about 70% of people suffering from manic-depressive illlnes.

153

Lloyd George, David: Prime Minister of England between 1916 and 1922, he should not be confused with David Lloyd, the Chief Justice of Pennsylvania between 1717 and 1731.

Loom: One of those machines that weaves thread into fabric.

Luddites: A group of workers who destroyed looms in England between 1811and 1816. Under the "leadership" of the probably mythical General Ned Ludd, the Luddites demanded better wages and working conditions and destroyed the looms in factories that failed to comply. On April 20, 1812, a large group of Luddites were prevented from destroying a particular factory and so burned the owner's house down instead, precipitating a government crackdown on Luddite activity. Contemporary Luddites shun technology, as you can see from their World Wide Web site at http://www.luddites.com/.

Lungs: Respiratory organs that can extract oxygen from air. Lungs probably developed about 420 million years ago in fishes and were used to breathe air at the surface of the water. This enabled the fish with lungs to swim faster and longer than the fish without lungs. Lungs later became extremely useful to the animals that left the ocean to live on land, where gills tend not to work very well.

Lutheranism: In 1517, Martin Luther felt compelled to protest the Catholic Church's granting of indulgences (pardons for pay). He nailed his 95 theses to the church door in Wittenberg and started down the path that would lead to the Protestant Reformation and eventually to Garrison Keillor. This is his religion, although he would have preferred it to have had a different name (Luther, not Keillor).

Luxembourg: The Grand Duchy of Luxembourg is located in western Europe between Belgium, France, and Germany. A land of gently rolling hills, Luxembourg enjoys a stable economy with a 4% growth rate, a 2% inflation rate, and a 3% unemployment rate. It exports steel products, chemicals,rubber products, glass, and aluminum, while importing minerals, metals,food, and consumer goods. The government is a constitutional monarchy whose head of state is a hereditary Grand Duke. Every 5 years all sixty members of the legislative Chamber of Deputies are elected by direct popular vote. Judges on the Superior Court of Justice are appointed for life by the Grand Duke. The dominant languages in Luxembourg are Luxembourgish, German, French, and English. Roman Catholicism is the prevailing religion. Luxembourg was made a duchy in 1354 by Holy Roman Emperor Charles IV. During the next 450 years, the duchy was claimed atone time or another by France, the Netherlands, Austria, and Spain. In 1815 it was made a grand duchy, and during the next 50 years it was claimed by the Netherlands, Germany, Belgium, and France. In 1867 it was declared a neutral territory. Germany occupied the grand duchy between 1914 and 1918 and between 1940 and 1944. A constitutional revision in 1948 revoked the perpetual neutrality of the grand duchy. Luxembourg is a member of the European Union and is closely connected economically to the Netherlands and especially to Belgium. The Luxembourg franc is fixed to the Belgian franc, and Belgian francs circulate freely in Luxembourg.

Macumba: Based on the spirit worship of Africans shipped to Brazil in the 1550s as slaves, Macumba teaches that humans have both a physical and a spiritual body, that the physical world is always being contacted by spirits, and that humans can learn to contact spirits for the purposes of healing and spiritual evolution.

Magnetic field: Caused by the electromagnetic force, these fields affect moving charged particles and are responsible for magnetism and, indirectly, for ATM cards.

Magnetic monopoles: All magnets have so-called north and south ends.Magnetic monopoles are theoretical particles that would be only north or only south. Many have searched for a monopole-derived Nobel Prize, but none have been successful so far.

Magnetism: What am I, a dictionary?

Manichaeism: Founded by the Persian sage Mani in the third century A.D..,this religion teaches that the human body is evil and that the soul can only be redeemed by conquering its carnal desires.

Marduk: The ruler of the Sumerian gods, he defeated Tiamat in battle and cut her in half to form the heavens and the earth. Afterwards he created people out of clay and produced seeds so that they could grow food.

Marquis: A nobleman of high rank. One ranking system goes king, duke, marquis, count, and baron, in decreasing order of royalness.

Marquise: A noblewoman of high rank. One ranking system goes: queen, duchess, marquise, countess, and baroness, in decreasing order of royalness.

Mars: The fourth planet from the Sun, its mass is 10% of the Earth's, and it is 4000 miles in diameter. Mars has a thin atmosphere of carbon dioxide,two small moons, and a tendency to attack the Earth in science fiction stories.

Martinism: Founded by Louis-Claude de Saint-Martin, Martinism teaches that one should not work for personal interest and that the sexes are equal in the ability to develop divine gifts.

McCormick, Cyrus Hall: This Virginia native invented the mechanical reaper at the age of 22 and, in so doing, set the world on the path to modern agriculture.

Mechanical reaper: A machine that allowed the harvesting of crops as soon as they were ripe, it solved one of the most important farming problems.Until the mechanical reaper, crop losses were large because harvesting took too long and was too inefficient.

Mennonites: Founded in 1526 as a sect of the Anabaptist faith, Mennonite churches exist as associations of people who are mature enough to make free-will decisions to join the church. People who seem to deviate from the teachings of the church are banned from the congregation and shunned.

Mercury: The closest planet to the Sun, its mass is 6% of the Earth's, and it is 3000 miles in diameter. Mercury has a very thin atmosphere of sodium gas. Mercury is also the name of a chemical element used in many thermometers, some batteries, but few reputable hair care products.

Methane: A molecule composed of one atom of carbon and four atoms of hydrogen. On Earth, a colorless, odorless, flammable gas that can be obtained from marshes, natural gas, and cattle (do I have to spell it out?). It is a greenhouse gas.

Methodism: A Protestant Christian movement started by John Wesley in1729. Conversion is central to Methodism, as is repentance, faith,sanctification, and the privilege of salvation for everyone.

Michel, John: Senior Editor at W. H. Freeman and Company Publishers and source of good ideas and helpful advice.

Microscopic organisms: Organisms that one needs a microscope to see. These organisms are very small compared to the size of a wombat, for example.

Microsporidian: A protozoan organism that forms spores for reproduction or for protection when the environment turns hostile.

Military commissioned officer ranks: In the U.S. Army, Air Force, and Marine Corps, the commissioned officer ranks go as follows: second lieutenant, first lieutenant, captain, major, lieutenant colonel, colonel,brigadier general, major general, lieutenant general, and general. Note that a major outranks a lieutenant, but that a lieutenant general outranks a major general. In the U. S. Navy, the commissioned officer ranks go as follows: ensign, lieutenant (junior grade), lieutenant commander, commander, captain, rear admiral, vice admiral, and admiral. Note that in the U. S. Navy a captain is a relatively high ranking officer, while in the other U. S.military services, a captain is a relatively low ranking officer. In the German Infantry and Air Force, the commissioned officer ranks go as follows:leutnant, oberleutnant, hauptmann, stabshauptmann, major, oberstleutnant,obserst, brigadegeneral, generalmajor, generalleutnant, and general. In the German Navy, the commissioned officer ranks go as follows: leutnant zur see,oberleutnant zur see, kapitänleutnant, stabskapitänleutnant, korvettenkapitän,fregattenkapitän, kapitän zur see, flottillenadmiral, konteradmiral,vizeadmiral, and admiral. In the British Royal Air Force, the officer ranks go as follows: pilot officer, flying officer, flying lieutenant, squadron leader, wing commander, group captain, air commodore, air vice-marshal, air marshal, and air chief marshal. Of course, there are also enlisted ranks,non-commissioned officer ranks, other countries, and other services, some of which have not existed for thousands of years, and some of which are not scheduled to exist until hundreds of years from now, but this is supposed to be a concise glossary entry so they must of necessity be omitted here.

Mithraism: One of the dominant religions of the Roman Empire, Mithraism was centered on the struggle between the forces of good and evil. Mithraic ceremonies included fasting and secret rituals including baptism.

Mole: 6.0221367×10^{23} of something. Also, a small burrowing mammal with tiny eyes.

Molecule: A collection of atoms held together by electromagnetic forces.

Mole of Moles: 6.0221367×10^{23} small burrowing mammals.

Mollusks: A diverse phylum of invertebrate animals that includes snails, squids, clams, and a large number of other organisms. Note that it does not include the brachiopods, which really are quite different from clams. For one thing, the two shell valves in brachiopods are often unequal in size, whereas the two shell valves in most clams are the same size. See, I told you I'd get back to you on this.

Molybdenum: Molybdenum nuclei have 42 protons and usually 54 neutrons. On Earth it is a white metal often used in alloys that need to stand up to high temperatures (jet engine turbines, for example).

Momentum: A quantity equal to the mass of the body multiplied by its velocity. A 1-ton truck traveling at 60 mph has more momentum than a 5-ton truck traveling at 5 mph, but you wouldn't want either of them (or anything else, for that matter) to run into your Miata.

Monica: In Roman Catholicism, the patron saint of married women.

Moon: An object that orbits around a planet and is larger than about 10 miles in diameter. Mercury and Venus have no moons, Earth and Pluto have one each, Mars has two, and Jupiter, Saturn, Uranus, and Neptune have dozens.

Mormonism: Founded in 1830 by Joseph Smith, the Church of Jesus Christ of Latter-Day Saints teaches that people live as spirit beings with God before being born, that life on Earth serves as a test to determine whether people are worthy to return to God, and that the spiritual body is judged after death and if worthy is placed into one of three Heavens, depending on worthiness. Mormons perform baptisms for the dead and participate in the Church's extensive missionary program.

Mouse: A small shrew-like animal with a thin tail.

Multicellular organism: An organism composed of a number of different kinds of cells. My guess is that you are a multicellular organism.

Mysticism: A broad spectrum of beliefs that center on putting oneself into a direct relationship with God, Nature, or a unifying principle of life through personal religious experience. Many religions have mystical components.

Natural selection: The process of evolution by which organisms that are well-suited to their environment tend to live and reproduce themselves while those that are poorly suited tend to die off before reproducing.

Neo-Paganism: Founded in 1951 by Gerald B. Gardner, Neo-Paganism, or Wicca, worships the sacredness of nature, teaches that one must have balance in life, and draws much of its inspiration from ancient European religions. There are few strict rules; people are allowed to do what they will so long as no harm befalls others or themselves. Neo-Paganism now includes many other belief systems besides Wicca.

Neoplatonism: Founded by the Roman philosopher Plotinus, this set of philosophical and religious beliefs teaches that pure intelligence emanates from a perfect unknowable One that gives each soul a choice between a sensual and corrupt existence or self-denial that will eventually lead to an all-pervading ecstasy. Neoplatonists recommend the latter.

Neptune: Usually the eighth planet from the Sun (sometimes Pluto is closer), it has 17 times the mass of the Earth, and it is 30,000 miles in diameter. Neptune has a thick atmosphere composed mostly of hydrogen and helium. It has about ten moons larger than 30 miles in diameter.Neptune does not appear to be intrinsically amusing.

Netherlands, The: A country in western Europe. See the entry on Holland.

Neutrino: A chargeless but probably not massless particle required by many particle interactions that use the weak nuclear force. Hair-care products almost always contain neutrinos, but these neutrinos are replaced with new ones every 100 billionth of a second on average. This may be one reason why hair-care products are so expensive these days.

Neutrons: These particles have no charge and are found in the nuclei of atoms and in almost every hair-care product on the market today.

Neutron star: Composed entirely of neutrons, these objects are more massive than the Sun and are about 20 miles across. Stars more massive than about eight times the mass of the Sun will probably end their lives as neutron stars, or perhaps black holes.

News group: A series of messages devoted to a particular topic that is transmitted over Usenet, a distributed network of more than 75,000 computers.

Ninki: In Sumerian cosmology she was married the god Enki; Marduk was their son.

Nitrogen: Nitrogen nuclei have seven protons and usually seven neutrons. On Earth,a colorless, odorless gas. Nitrogen atoms are an important component of proteins, nucleic acids, and gunpowder—and hair-care products.

Nixon, Richard Milhous: Even though the FBI turned him down for a job after he graduated from law school, he went on to become President of the United States (1969-1974).

Nobel Prize: This prize honors people whose achievements have conferred great benefit on humanity in the fields of physics, chemistry, physiology or medicine, literature, peace, and economics. They are even more highly sought after than Ig(R) Nobel Prizes.

Noetzli, Regula: Affiliate of the Charlotte Sheedy Literary Agency, and expert negotiator.

North America: A continent in the northern hemisphere of the planet Earth.

Nucleic acid: Nucleic acids like DNA (deoxyribonucleic acid) and RNA (ribonucleic acid) hold genetic information, facilitate protein synthesis in cells, and usually manage to increase profit margins for hair care products.

Occultism: The belief that hidden knowledge about mysterious forces that rule the universe can be tapped through supernatural means. Some believe that occult forces can cause 18 1/2-minute gaps in taped conversations.

Oneida: The Oneida Community was founded in 1848 by John Humphrey Noyes in a schism from Methodism and Adventism; it taught that right conduct must be based on love of God and encouraged group marriage and a scientific breeding program.

Organelle: A subcellular entity with specific duties. For example, mitochondria are organelles that perform respiration, while chloroplasts are organelles that perform photosynthesis.

Organic molecules: A class of chemical compounds that contain carbon and are essential to life as we know it, as well as to many hair-care products.

Oxygen: Oxygen nuclei have eight protons and usually eight neutrons. On Earth, a colorless, odorless gas that is produced by photosynthesis and is required for aerobic respiration, combustion, and the vast majority of hair-care products.

Ozone: A molecule composed of three atoms of oxygen. On Earth, a colorless gas with a peculiar burnt odor that blocks ultraviolet radiation.

Padua: Also known as Padova, it is a city in northern Italy.

Paganism: A broad spectrum of belief systems that include reverence for the Earth and all its creatures and generally see all life as interconnected.

Pantheism: A belief system that says that the Universe is God and that God is the Universe.

PCI BIOS: You don't want to know, and neither do I.

Pennsylvania: A state in the eastern United States.

Pentecostalism: Founded in 1901, this is the fastest-growing segment of Christianity in the world. The primary characteristics of Pentecostalism that differentiate it from other Christian denominations are speaking in tongues, prophesying, healings, and exorcism.

Perfidy: A violation of trust, such as using a competitor's hair-care products.

Phonograph record: These items used to be very popular for storing music. Think of them as large black compact disks where the music is read by a needle that moves in a groove.

Photons: Individual "particles" of light, photons have properties of both waves and particles. See the entry on quantum mechanics.

Photosynthesis: The process by which plants convert light, water, and carbon dioxide into carbohydrates and oxygen. In plants, this occurs in organelles called chloroplasts.

Pittsburgh: A city in western Pennsylvania.

Planet: A large body that orbits a star and does not produce energy by fusion reactions. In our solar system, planets range from 0.3% of the Earth's mass (Pluto) to 320 times the mass of the Earth (Jupiter). Planets around other stars have been discovered with masses up to 10 times the mass of Jupiter.

Platypus: A small egg-laying mammal with webbed feet and a duck-like bill.

Pluto: Usually the ninth planet from the Sun (sometimes Neptune is farther), its mass is 0.3% of the Earth's, and it is 1400 miles in diameter. Pluto has a thin atmosphere of nitrogen and a large moon. In 1999, the International Astronomical Union decided not to revoke Pluto's status as a planet. They also failed to pass a censure resolution against it.

Plutonium: Plutonium nuclei have 94 protons and usually between 144 (Pu-238)and 150 (Pu-244) neutrons. On Earth it is a radioactive metallic element used in atomic weapons and nuclear power plants. Do not buy hair care products that advertise a high plutonium content.

Polemics: The use of aggressive arguments in debates on controversial issues,such as which hair-care products are better than others.

Polonium: Polonium nuclei have 84 protons and usually 126 neutrons. On Earth it is a radioactive metallic element that is sometimes used with beryllium as a neutron source in atomic weapons.

Polytheism: Any belief system that includes a plurality of gods, especially when each has a special function. Polytheistic religions include those of ancient Egypt, Greece, Rome, India, and many others.

Possum: A marsupial that usually lives in trees.

Prairie dog: A small, burrowing rodent.

Presbyterianism: An organization of Christian churches that are governed by a hierarchy of courts rather than by bishops or by the individual congregations themselves.

Protein: The building blocks of life, proteins act as enzymes to catalyze reactions, as regulatory hormones, as intracellular membranes, and as antibodies, they also serve a variety of other purposes (for example, the protein hemoglobin carries oxygen in your blood). Proteins are made up of amino acids and are often found in hair-care products.

Proterozoic: The geologic era between 2.5 billion and 544 million years ago.

Protists: A kingdom of eukaryotic organisms with neither a complex development from embryos nor extensive cell differentiation.

Protons: These are positively charged particles that are found in the nucleus of atoms and in almost all hair-care products.

Protoplasm: The semiliquid complex of proteins, water, and organic and inorganic compounds that makes up the insides of living cells.

Protozoa: A phylum of eukaryotic organisms that contains unicellular and colonial species.

Quakers: The Society of Friends was founded in 1650; they believe that no one is holier than anyone else, they do not observe baptism, they perform marriage ceremonies for both opposite-sex and same-sex marriages,and they forbid members to join the military or make oaths.

Quantum mechanics: Among other things, quantum mechanics says that you can never know exactly where a particle is or how fast it is going, that you can't put two identical particles too close together, and that almost everything has some probability of happening. Quantum mechanics often seems to have a lot to do with dead cats, or half-dead cats, or potentially dead cats, or something like that.

Quayle, James Danforth: Vice President of the United States between 1989 and1993, he should not be confused with John Fitzgerald Kennedy, the President of the United States between 1961 and 1963.

Radon: Radon nuclei have 86 protons and usually 136 neutrons. Radon is a radioactive gas with a half-life of 92 hours. It is sometimes found in the basements of homes but very rarely on the surfaces of stars.

Ramsey, William: With Baron Rayleigh, he discovered argon in 1894. With Nilo Langet and P. T. Cleve, he discovered helium in 1895. With M. W. Travers, he discovered neon, krypton, and xenon in 1898. He had a busy five years.

Rastafarianism: Founded in the 1930s, Rastafarians believe that His Imperial Majesty Haile Selassie I is the living God for the black race, that Ethiopia is Heaven on Earth, that there is no afterlife,and that blacks are held down through poverty, illiteracy, and inequality.

Reagan, Ronald Wilson: A successful American actor, his movie roles included George Armstrong Custer in *Santa Fe Trail* (1940), George Gipp in *Knute Rockne, All American* (1940), and Professor Peter Boyd in *Bedtime for Bonzo* (1951). He was President of the United States between 1981 and 1989.Not to be confused with his son, Ron Reagan, who played Frank in *Soul Man* (1986) and also appeared in the 1993 TV show *The Positively True Adventures of the Alleged Texas Cheerleader-Murdering Mom*.

Rear admiral: A relatively high-ranking naval officer. See the entry on military commissioned officer ranks.

Rec.humor.funny: An internet news group that distributes a few works of humor per day to half a million readers around the world.

Recursion: See the chapter on inscription.

Respiration: The process by which animals and plants convert carbohydrates and oxygen to energy, water, and carbon dioxide. This occurs in organelles called mitochondria.

Ribonucleic acid (RNA): The nucleic acid that facilitates protein synthesis for organisms on the Earth. The fundamental building blocks of RNA are a phosphate (PO_4), a sugar (ribose), and a nucleic acid base (either adenine,uracil, guanine, or cytosine). Some hair-care products have RNA in them.

Rodents: An order of mammals that feed by gnawing or nibbling.

Rodinia: A supercontinent that included almost all of the land masses of the world between 2.5 billion and about 500 million years ago.

Roebuck, Alvah: A watchmaker from Indiana who co-founded Sears, Roebuck and Company in 1893 with Richard Sears.

Rome: Known as "The City of Seven Hills," Rome was founded in 1834 where the Etowah and Oostanaula rivers meet. A bustling city of more than 30,000 people, Rome is the regional center for a six-county area that has a population of about a quarter of a million people. Rome is near the center of the triangle formed by Atlanta (Georgia), Birmingham (Alabama), and Chattanooga (Tennessee).

Roosevelt, Franklin Delano: President of the United States from 1933 until his death in 1945, he should not be confused with Theodore Roosevelt, who was President of the United States from 1901 until 1909. FDR was elected President of the United States in 1932, re-elected in 1936, and re-elected in 1940 after saying, "Your boys are not going to be sent into any foreign wars." Eleven months after his inauguration he asked Congress to declare war on Japan. He was re-elected to a fourth term as president in 1944.

Roosevelt, Theodore: President of the United States from 1901 until1909, he should not be confused with Franklin Delano Roosevelt, who was President of the United States from 1933 until 1945. I should also mention the Bull Moose party and the staggeringly important election of 1912, but I won't.

Rosicrucian Order: The Ancient Mystical Order Rosae Crucis was founded in 1915 by H. Spencer Lewis. Members study ancient and modern knowledge of science, mysticism, philosophy, and metaphysics.

Rutherford, Daniel: He discovered nitrogen in 1772.

Sagan, Carl: Astronomer, planetary scientist, author, winner of the Pulitzer Prize, and science popularizer extraordinaire. He died on December 20, 1996, at the age of 62.

Saint Vincent and the Grenadines: This band had a hit in 1963 with their rendition of "Unchained Melody." No, wait, that was Vito and the Salutations. Actually, the country of Saint Vincent and the Grenadines is 130 square miles of small Caribbean islands north of Trinidad and Tobago. Spain claimed the islands in the fifteenth and sixteenth centuries, and Britain and France did likewise in the seventeenth and eighteenth centuries; they were ceded to Britain in 1783, and they attained independence on October 27, 1979.

Salandra, Antonio: Premier of Italy between March of 1914 and June of 1916,he led his country into World War I.

162

Santeria: Founded in the 1700s, Santeria is a blend of West African religions and European Catholicism. Santerians believe in spirits (orishas)that are the emissaries of God, possess distinct personalities, and can be summoned through certain music, colors, and animals.

Satanism: Founded in 1966 by Anton Szandor LaVay, the Church of Satan teaches that people should devote their lives to fulfilling their desires and to helping others do the same.

Saturn: The sixth planet from the Sun, Saturn has 95 times the mass of the Earth and is 75,000 miles in diameter. It has about twenty moons larger than 10 miles in diameter and one moon larger than 3000 miles in diameter. Saturn's atmosphere is very thick and is composed almost entirely of hydrogen and helium. It has an extensive and beautiful system of rings.

Savannah: A grassy plain with few trees. Also a seaport in eastern Georgia. Also a grassy plain with few trees in eastern Georgia.

Sheele, Carl Wilhelm: He discovered oxygen in 1774 (independent of Joseph Priestly), Chlorine in 1774, and Molybdenum in 1778.

von Schlieffen, Count Alfred: Chief of the German General Staff from 1891until 1906, he borrowed a few ideas from Hannibal to create the Schlieffen plan for defeating France within six weeks. It didn't quite work out that way in World War I.

Scholasticism: A theological movement which taught that since God is the source of both revelation and reason; any apparent contradiction between the two was due either to an incorrect interpretation of revelation or to faulty reasoning.

Schrödinger's Cat: Put a cat in a box. Put a vial of poison gas in the box,along with one radioactive atom and a detector that will release the gas if the atom decays. Close the box. If the radioactive element has a half-life of an hour, then the laws of probability say that after sixty minutes the cat has a 50% chance of being alive and a 50% chance of being dead. Quantum mechanics, on the other hand, says that after an hour the cat is 50% alive and 50% dead. Only once you look inside the box will the cat become either 100% alive or 100% dead.

Schulman, Emily: Co-author of the *Annals of Improbable Research* article "How to Write a Scientific Research Report" and all-around amazing person.

Schulman, Eric: Author of *A Briefer History of Time*, contributor to *The Best of Annals of Improbable Research*, and member of the editorial board of the *Annals of Improbable Research*.

Schulman, Marvin: Teacher, legislative field agent, expert on history and politics, and inspirational father.

Scientific notation: A system for writing very large or very small numbers compactly. 10^{30} is scientific notation for the number that can is expressed as a 1 followed by 30 zeros in ordinary decimal notation: 1000000000000000000000000000000. 3 X 10^{-35} is scientific notation for the number that can be expressed as a decimal point followed by 34 zeros and a three: 0.00000000000000000000000000000000003.See why scientific notation was invented?

Scientific Pantheism: Founded in 1995 by Paul Harrison, this belief system attempts to combine religion and science into a coherent whole.

Scientology: The Church of Scientology was founded in 1954 by science fiction author L. Ron Hubbard.

Scots: A group of people from Ireland who settled in Scotland in about 500 A.D.

Sears, Richard: A Professor of Astronomy at the University of Michigan in Ann Arbor, he co-founded Sears, Roebuck and Company with Alvah Roebuck in 1893. On second thought, it's possible that that was a different Richard Sears.

Seicho-No-Ie: Founded in 1930 by Dr. Masaharu Taniguchi, this movement believes that all religions emanate from one universal God and that every person has all the creative powers of God.

Serpent Handlers: Founded in about 1908, the Church of God with Signs Following derives from the Pentecostal movement and believes that it is important to speak with new tongues, take up serpents, and lay hands on the sick (based on the Bible, especially Mark 16:17-18).

Seventh-Day Adventists: Officially organized in 1863, Seventh-Day Adventists believe that the Second Coming of Jesus Christ will occur soon. They believe that the human body is a temple to God and so do not smoke, drink alcohol, or use drugs.

Shakers: The United Society of Believers splintered off from a Quaker community in 1772. Shakers emphasized celibacy and simplicity in their daily lives and believed that God is a duality of male and female rather than a trinity.

Shamanism: Any of a number of belief systems that include the idea that the world is pervaded by spirits that affect the living and that these spirits can be contacted by shamans. Shamanism is found in Native American,African, Inuit, and Siberian religions.

Shinto: The ancient native religion of Japan, in which a large number of generally beneficent supernatural beings, or *kami,* oversee the world.

Shirdi Sai Baba: Founded in 1940 by Sathya Sai Baba, this sect of Hinduism believes that there is one God who is called different names by different religions; only unreligious people are wrong. Sai Baba followers strive to achieve enlightenment by having pious faith and directing all thoughts,feelings, and actions toward God.

Shrew: A small, mouse-like animal with a long snout.

Silicon: Silicon nuclei have 14 protons and usually 14 neutrons. On Earth, a metallic element used in semiconductors and glass. There's probably some silicon in your favorite hair care product.

Simpson, Orenthal James: OJ Simpson was born in 1947 and has worked as a football player, a TV and movie actor, and a TV producer at different stages in his career.

Singer, Isaac Bashevis: A Polish-born American writer who was awarded the Nobel Prize for literature in 1978, he should not be confused with the Isaac Singer who patented the sewing machine in 1851

Singer, Isaac Merrit: An American inventor who patented the sewing machine in 1851. He lost a patent infringement suit brought by Elias Howe but in spite of this his company went on to become rather successful. He should not be confused with the Isaac Singer who was awarded the Nobel Prize for literature in 1978.

Sikhism: Founded in about 1500 A.D., Sikhism combines Hindu and Moslem ideas. Sikhs believe in monotheism, that all religions are one, and that God can be realized through meditation and religious exercises.

Skepticism: The belief that one can never know what to believe.

Solar mass: The mass of Earth's sun, which is equivalent to 4000 billion billion billion pounds. That's a big number, but perhaps we can make it more manageable by converting from pounds to elephant masses. An elephant can weigh 16,000 pounds, so it would take only 250 million billion billion elephants to have the same mass as the Sun. I guess that didn't help very much.

Solar system: A system of planets orbiting around one or more stars. We are in a solar system composed of the Sun, nine planets including the Earth, and thousands of smaller objects such as moons, asteroids, and comets.

Solid: A state of matter in which the volume and the shape tend to be constant. This book is solid. If it should be turned into a liquid or a gas, then you will be unable to read it anymore and should immediately go out and buy another copy (and perhaps a spare or two in case it happens again).

Spain: A country in southwestern Europe.

Spinning Jenny: The first mechanical spinner, it allowed carded cotton to be spun into thread automatically, multiplying the productivity of workers by a factor of 8

Spiritism: Founded in the 1850s by Allan Kardec (the nom de plume of H. Leon Denizard Rivail), spiritists believe that mediums can communicate with spirits that will answer philosophical and scientific questions.

Spiritualism: Founded by Emanuel Swedenborg in 1744, this movement believes that the spirit world overlaps with the material world and that the spirits of the dead can communicate with the living. Other beliefs include the infinite nature of God, that service to others improves one's spirit, that the soul exists for eternity, and that people are responsible for their own thoughts and actions.

Sponges: Sponges were among the first animals to develop. They feed by filtering water that is drawn through their pores and expelled out through larger openings. Sponges are handy to have in the kitchen.

Squirrel: A bushy-tailed rodent that lives in trees and gathers nuts.

Sri Chinmoy: Founded in 1964 by Chinmoy Kumar Ghose (now known as Sri Chinmoy) as an offshoot from Hinduism, this movement tries to attain personal harmony, international harmony, and world peace through meditation, living and working in the world, vegetarianism, and celibacy.

Stalin, Joseph Vissarionovich: Born Iosif Vissarionovich Dzhugashvili, he was a divinity student (expelled for political activities in 1898), a bank robber (in T'bilisi in 1907), and a newspaper founder (*Pravda* in 1911).He was also the General Secretary of the Central Committee of the Communist Party of the Union of Soviet Socialist Republics from 1922 until his death in 1953.

Star: A stable sphere of mostly hydrogen and helium gas supported against gravitational collapse by nuclear fusion in the core. At a distance of roughly 93 million miles, the Sun is the nearest star to the Earth.

Starch: A carbohydrate made up of many molecules of glucose. Starches are often found in hair-care products.

Stereoisomer: A molecule that is composed of the same atoms as another molecule, but arranged in a way that makes each molecule the mirror image of the other. Also, a device that allows you to listen to music while strengthening your muscles—or was that an isometrics stereo?

Stoicism: Founded in about 300 B.C. by Zeno, this belief system taught that each human soul is part of a universal divine power, and that everyone should aspire to be wise, courageous, just, and temperant, and should love and help one another regardless of social class.

Strong nuclear force: One of the four fundamental forces of nature, this force holds the nucleus of atoms together and is very important for the stability of hair-care products.

Subduction: The process by which oceanic crust is pushed under either oceanic or continental crust, usually resulting in volcanic activity as the newly melted rock makes its way toward the surface.

Sufism: Developed in the late tenth century A.D. within Islam, this mystical movement emphasizes a personal union of the soul with God, often through ascetic practices.

Sugar: Sweet carbohydrates such as glucose ($C_6 H_{12} O_6$) or sucrose ($C_{12} H_{22} O_{11}$) that are sometimes found in hair-care products and often found in cookies.

Sulfuric acid: A molecule composed of one atom of sulfur, four atoms of oxygen, and two atoms of hydrogen. On Earth, sulfuric acid is an oily,corrosive liquid that is rarely found in reputable hair-care products.

Suma Ching Hai: Founded in 1982 by Hue Dang Trinh (now known as Suma Ching Hai), this movement combines Christianity and Buddhism. Followers meditate for 2 1/2 hours per day and refrain from taking the life of sentient beings, speaking what is not true, taking what is not offered, sexual misconduct, and using intoxicants.

Supercluster of galaxies: A group of dozens of clusters of galaxies that is held together by gravitational attraction.

Swift, Jonathan: This Irish author is most famous for his 1726 work, *Travels into Several Remote Nations of the World.*

Symbiosis: Mutual cooperation between different organisms such that each benefit from the relationship.

Synanon Church: Founded in 1958 by Charles E. Dederich, this movement seeks to manifest oneness by combining beliefs from Buddhism, Taoism, Emerson, and Aldous Huxley.

Taoism: Founded by Lao-tze in the sixth century B.C., this philosophical religion teaches that the ideal state of being is freedom from desire,which can only be reached through mystical contemplation. People who are one with the Tao (the way the universe functions) act through effortless action.

Tapir: A large, usually inoffensive, chiefly nocturnal hoofed mammal with a long, flexible snout. Tapir are cool, but it's best to be cautious around a mother tapir and her two-month-old baby.

Temperant: Having self-restraint, especially in regard to the consumption of alcoholic beverages.

Tenrikyo: Founded in 1838 by Miki Nakayama (now known as Oyasama), this movement believes that God created human beings in order that they would live joyous lives by helping and respecting others and by making them happy.

Tethys Sea: A tropical sea that existed hundreds of millions of years ago.

Tetrapod: A group of four-legged vertebrates including amphibians, dinosaurs,birds, and mammals. Most of the readers of this book are probably tetrapods.

The: The definite article of the English language, which gives particulars for the noun it modifies. Or something like that.

Theosophy: Founded in 1875 by Helen Petrovna Blavatsky, this pantheistic movement believes in "the unity of life, the law of cycles, and the progressive unfoldment of consciousness in all kingdoms of nature."

Tiamat: In Sumerian cosmology Tiamat was a dragon goddess who lived in the sea. After one of the gods complained that the others were making too much noise, she gave birth to a host of strange creatures (lion-demons, scorpion-men, sphinxes, mad dogs, etc.) and sent them out to make the gods behave themselves. The gods were a bit shaken by this army and promised Marduk that he could have supreme authority over everything if he would just take care of this little problem for them. Marduk agreed to the deal,slew Tiamat, and created the heavens and the earth out of her dead body.

Tocqueville, Alexis Charles Henri Maurice Clérel de: This French politician wrote an often-quoted book about America and went on to become the vice president of the French National Assembly in 1849.

Transcendentalism: First espoused by Plato in the fourth century B.C., this belief system teaches that divinity permeates all objects and that although absolute goodness exists, it is only knowable through intuition rather than through human experience or reason.

Transcendental Meditation: Founded in 1956 by Mehesh Prasad Varma (now known as Maharishi Mahesh Yogi), this Hindu movement teaches that people can reach an enlightened state through meditation, which will lead to increased intelligence, higher levels of resistance to disease, and better job performance.

Trichomonad: A unicellular organism with multiple flagella.

Trigoencephalopodic gnocci: I made this one up.

Trilobites: Trilobites were an extremely successful subphylum of the arthropods that were at the top of the food chain in Earth's marine ecosystems for about 250 million years.

Tsunami: A very big wave, also known as a tidal wave, which can be caused by earthquakes or asteroid impacts, although not by tides.

Tunneling: Quantum mechanics says that the position of a particle is uncertain, and therefore that there is some possibility that a particle will be within an energy barrier rather than outside of it. The process of moving from outside to inside without traversing the distance between is known as quantum tunneling, and it is very important for the fusion reactions in stars like the Sun.

Ubiquitous: Seeming to exist everywhere at once.

Ultraviolet light: UV light is made up of photons that are more energetic than those that we can see (visible light). On Earth, most UV light from the Sun is blocked by the ozone layer (for now, at least). UV photons are energetic enough to cause cell damage and promote skin cancer.

Unicellular organism: A life form composed of only one cell.

Unification Church: The Holy Spirit Association for the Unification of World Christianity was founded in 1954 by Sun Myung Moon. It teaches that people can be restored from sin by recognizing Moon's special status, joining the Unification movement, raising money and winning converts for the Unification Church, receiving Moon's blessing in marriage, bearing sinless children, and leading lives that will produce a sinless world.

Unitarian Universalism: Founded in 1961 as a merger between the Unitarian and Universalist Christian traditions, this movement believes that God is the author of reason and religion, that all religions have a right to their own beliefs, and that no two people see the truth in the same way.

United States: A country in central North America.

Universe: The Universe is a three-dimensional volume of space that may or may not be infinite in size. At the very least it is quite large. To be more specific, it is almost certainly larger than a billion billion billion billion billion billion billion billion billion cubic yards. To put that in perspective, the volume of the Earth is only a thousand billion billion cubic yards, while the volume of the Galaxy is about a billion billion billion billion billion billion billion cubic yards.If you think about it, you will conclude that the Universe is staggeringly huge compared to the Galaxy, which is colossal when compared to the Earth, which is gigantic when compared to you. My advice is not to think about it too much.

Uranium: Uranium nuclei have 92 protons and usually either 143 neutrons (U-235) or 146 neutrons (U-238). On Earth, a radioactive metallic element used in atomic weapons and nuclear power plants but rarely if ever in hair-care products.

Uranus: The seventh planet from the Sun, it has fifteen times the mass of the Earth and is 30,000 miles in diameter. Uranus has a thick atmosphere composed mostly of hydrogen and helium. It has about fifteen moons larger than 15 miles in diameter. Jokes about Uranus tend to be in poor taste.

Urantia: The Urantia Brotherhood was founded in the early 195's by Dr. William S. Sadler. It teaches that Urantia is an ancient name for the planet Earth, that Jesus is the sovereign of Earth's (Urantia's) local universe, and that God the Universal Father is present in all universes, which are each guided by a different Son of God.

Vacuum energy density: You just had to ask, didn't you? OK, here goes. Quantum mechanics says that there is a non-zero probability of a particle-antiparticle pair being created and destroyed in a given volume of space in a given period of time. From one point of view, these particles and antiparticles don't really exist because they are created from nothing and go back to nothing in a very short period of time. However, while they are there they do have mass and energy, so even though they are "virtual" particles, they contribute to the energy density of space. If the "vacuum" energy density is very large then

169

the universe can expand exponentially, and this is thought to have happened during the inflationary period very soon after the Big Bang.

Venus: The second planet from the Sun, its mass is 80% of that of the Earth, and its diameter is 7500 miles. It has a thick atmosphere of carbon dioxide. Venus very rarely attacks the Earth in science fiction stories.

Verona: A city in northern Italy.

Violent relaxation: You don't want to know. Sounds like a cool album name though, doesn't it?

Virialization: You *really* don't want to know. But this could be the name of the band.

Virus: In biology, a virus is an entity that can only reproduce itself within a host cell. Since viruses reproduce they can be thought of as alive, but since they don't grow, move, or eat, they can be thought of as not-alive.Viruses are like Schrödinger's Cat in that way. In computer science, a virus is a program that inserts copies of itself into other programs and usually causes some (potentially undesirable) even to happen, sometimes on a given date.

Volatile: A material that evaporates rapidly under prevailing conditions.

Volcano: An opening in the crust of the Earth through which liquid rock escapes to the surface.

Water: Dihydrogen monoxide is a molecule composed of two atoms of hydrogen and one atom of oxygen. It is produced by photosynthesis and required for respiration. On Earth it is an odorless, tasteless, colorless liquid that may react vigorously with certain materials.

Weak nuclear force: One of the four fundamental forces of nature, this force changes particles into other particles. For example, in nuclear fusion, protons are changed into neutrons via the weak nuclear force.

White dwarf: An object with the mass of the Sun and the size of the Earth. Stars less massive than about 8 solar masses will end their lives as white dwarfs.

Wilhelm II: Born in 1859 and becoming King of Prussia and German Kaiser in 1888,he got Germany into war in 1914. World War I did not go well for Germany, however, and on November 9, 1918, Germany became a republic and the dynasty that had ruled for 300 years was over. The Kaiser fled to the Netherlands and wrote his memoirs, in which he tried to convince the world that World War I hadn't been his fault.

Wilson, Woodrow: The first—and so far only—President of the United States to have earned a Ph.D., Dr. Wilson was elected president in 1912 and re-elected in 1916 using the campaign slogan "he kept us out of war." Three months after his inauguration he asked Congress to declare war on Germany.

Wombat: An Australian marsupial with short legs and a small tail.

Yeltsin, Boris Nikolayevich: An excellent high school volleyball player who went on to become President of Russia.

Zoroastrianism: Founded by Zarathustra (also known as Zoroaster) in about 630 B.C., this Persian religion believes in one supreme God named Ahura Mazda who created all things. There is also an evil spirit named Angra Mainyu and humans must choose to serve one side or the other. This choice may be helped by the knowledge that Ahura Mazda will triumph in the end.

Zuckerman, Benjamin: Professor of physics and astronomy at UCLA, editor of the book "Extraterrestrials, Where Are They?", and inspirational teacher of "Life in the Universe."